ENGLISH LANGUAGE SERIES

TITLE NO 16

The language of humour

ENGLISH LANGUAGE SERIES
General Editor: Randolph Quirk

Title no:

INVESTIGATING ENGLISH STYLE 1
David Crystal and Derek Davy

THE MOVEMENT OF ENGLISH PROSE 2
Ian A. Gordon

A LINGUISTIC GUIDE TO ENGLISH POETRY 4
Geoffrey N. Leech

AN INTRODUCTION TO 7
MODERN ENGLISH WORD-FORMATION
Valerie Adams

COHESION IN ENGLISH 9
M. A. K. Halliday and Ruqaiya Hasan

AN INTRODUCTION TO ENGLISH 10
TRANSFORMATIONAL SYNTAX
Rodney Huddleston

MEANING AND FORM 11
Dwight Bolinger

DESIGNS IN PROSE 12
Walter Nash

STYLE IN FICTION 13
Geoffrey N. Leech and Michael H. Short

THE RHYTHMS OF ENGLISH POETRY 14
Derek Attridge

MESSAGE AND EMPHASIS 15
Josef Taglisht

THE LANGUAGE OF HUMOUR 16
Walter Nash

The language of humour

WALTER NASH
Senior Lecturer in English Studies,
University of Nottingham

Foreword by Randolph Quirk

LONGMAN
London and New York

LONGMAN GROUP LIMITED
Longman House, Burnt Mill, Harlow
Essex CM20 2JE, England
Associated companies throughout the world

Published in the United States of America
by Longman Inc., New York

First published 1985

British Library Cataloguing in Publication Data
Nash, Walter, 1926 –
The language of humour.—(English language series; no. 16)
1. English wit and humor—History and criticism 2. English language—Style
I. Title II. Series
827'.009 PR931
ISBN 0-582-29127-5

Library of Congress Cataloging in Publication Data
Nash, Walter.
The language of humour.

(English language series; 16)
Bibliography: p.
Includes index.
1. English wit and humor—History and criticism.
2. English language—Style. 3. Style, Literary.
3. Comic, The. I. Title. II. Series.
PR931.N37 1985 808.7 84-12631
ISBN 0-582-29127-5

Set in Linotron 202 10/12pt Times
Printed in Singapore by
Selector Printing Co Pte Ltd

Contents

Foreword

From the time that the English Language Series was launched in the mid 1960s, it has been my ambition to include a volume exploring the ways in which language resources are exploited to create or enhance wit, amusement, laughter. For long I was dissuaded from pursuing such a venture. 'A couple of hundred pages analysing humour,' I was repeatedly warned, 'and your readers will never smile again.'

The hazards of taking a poem to pieces are bad enough. Will it ever work again when it is re-assembled? The most admirable and highly motivated critical purposes can be frustrated in the critic's dissecting room.

It may seem absurd to display comparable anxieties over the danger of fatality to a joke. On the one hand, we may feel that jokes are surely organisms with a great deal of rude robustness, of less delicate constitution than a lyric. Alternatively (and almost as a corollary) are jokes actually worth the effort and skill of the dissector's art? Do we need, in particular, to worry about life-support systems? That is, to switch the metaphor again from organism to machine, not only may the act of dismantling reveal merely an array of uninteresting components but we would scarcely wish to re-assemble a toy which cannot (unlike a lyric) repeat the joy it could of its nature evoke but once.

In fact, the premises of the preceding paragraph are multiply false. In the first place, there is a similar degree of delicate art in the well-formed joke and the well-formed poem. And both – the products of Ogden Nash and Ted Hughes, of Perelman and Frost – yield fresh enjoyment on re-acquaintance. Above all, at least under the hand of Walter Nash, the revelations of analysis are rewarding to the observer and actually breathe fresh life into what has been analysed.

This is partly because Dr Nash has the essential lightness of touch to handle such gossamer without misplacing a single thread. Partly because his wide and deep acquaintance with so vast a range of fabrics enriches his every act of criticism. But chiefly because he is not 'merely' a linguist and critic, expert in the theories informing analytical procedures (though, in all conscience, these skills cry out at the insult of 'merely'): he is even more centrally a creator than an analyst. This attribute embues him with the appropriate respect for and understanding of the art forms he is explicating. Indeed, many of the examples that so exquisitely illustrate his theoretical points are (unobtrusively, of course) from his own agile mind.

In my Foreword to his earlier volume in this series (*Designs in Prose*, 1980) I wrote: 'Though quite unjustifiably shy about his own achievements, Dr Nash is fortunate in possessing a highly creative imagination, both playful and profound, as those know well who are privileged to enjoy the poems, stories, and witty parodies he never bothers to publish.' It is no small part of my satisfaction with the present book that he was been confronted with a piece of writing in which he could scarcely do other than 'bother to publish' artefacts of his own, so uniquely fitted to his purpose.

So we have at last achieved the superb treatment of 'English for Fun' we have needed in this series. As English has increasingly come into world-wide use, there has arisen a correspondingly increasing need for more information on the language and the ways in which it is used. The English Language Series seeks to meet this need and to play a part in further stimulating the study and teaching of English by providing up-to-date and scholarly treatments of topics most relevant to the present-day language. And these include its history and traditions, its sound patterns, its grammar, its lexicology, its rich variety and complexity in speech and writing, and its standards in Britain, the USA, and the other principal areas of the world where the language is used.

University College London RANDOLPH QUIRK
June 1984

Preface

I assured myself that by the time I had finished this book I would never want to hear another joke, let alone make one. Such humbug. Not want to hear another joke? I am more than ever greedy for laughter, and grateful to those who create it; and I still have my wistful ambitions to make others smile. All that has happened is that an avuncular worldliness now tinges my attitude to humour. Having dismantled its mechanisms and rehearsed its paradigms, I think I know how things are put together; and the penalty of all knowledge is the loss of surprise.

I have been struck by the complexity of the subject – by the realization of what we are required to know, what social competence we must possess, what intellectual operations we may have to perform before we can grasp even a simple joke. I do not mean that you have to be Wittgenstein before you can grapple with a pun; only, that if you are about to converse with wits you must have your wits about you.

The fact is that, in humour, the diversities of our living and thinking tumble together in patterns adventitious and freakish and elegant, like the elaborate conformations of a kaleidoscope. In trying to describe intricacies of humorous *con*formation, I have borne constantly in mind three *in*forming principles: the workings of our language, the varieties of our social experience, and our habitual modes of thought. Each of these is so intimately involved with the others as to defy abstraction for the purposes of analysis. My commission, however, was to write a book on the *language* of humour, and I have accordingly tried to give the linguistic principle pride of place. In doing so, I have interpreted my brief quite broadly, endeavouring to set humorous language in the larger context of comic *style*. This concern with stylistic matters has directed the programme summarized in §1.6 and §2.9; I trust that as the reader proceeds from chapter to chapter the development of the argument will become clear to him.

Obviously, a book such as this requires copious illustration. My examples (excluding my own inventions) are of two main kinds. From the general public stock I have taken or adapted many brief jokes – quips, riddles, slogans, epigrams, aphorisms, things told in bars, propounded by clever children, or inscribed here and there on learned walls. It would be absurd to try to document such things with academic precision, though in my bibliography I mention one or two collections of folk humour to which I am casually indebted. The other kind of illustration uses passages from well-known works of humour and comedy. These passages came more or less readily to hand, as necessities of composition, and it is only on completing the book that I begin to feel uneasy about good things ignored or excluded. So many of my own favourite authors, so many examples that I would have thought indispensable, are not cited here. To the reader who might feel prompted to recite his own catalogue of grievous omissions, I would only say that my primary object has not been to make an annotated anthology of the finest jokes, the funniest poems, the best-loved comic episodes. Rather, it has been to outline *topics*, in a linguistic/stylistic domain, for which apposite illustrations had to be found. The process was often simple, not to say banal. One book rather than another happened to be on my shelves; the library could not immediately oblige me; something recently read was therefore freshly remembered. At times it may well have been convenient to forget treasured things – for so one keeps one's treasures.

Two problems in particular have bedevilled the composition of what I had hoped might be a lucid and urbanely discursive text: the transience of day-to-day humour, and the necessity of *explication*. Much excellent wit is a response to passing events, or is consumer fun for the consumer culture of advertisements, publicity, television, sport, popular journalism. When wit's object slides into history – with the helter-skelter haste of modern happenings – the wit itself requires annotation. In quite a large number of instances red-hot topicality has gone stone-cold while composition was still in progress, and I have been faced with the question, to annotate elaborately or to discard? In general, I have been encouraged to discard the 'dated' witticism, but I have stubbornly persisted in retaining two or three of these jokes, to have at hand some examples of the importance of the topicality that enlivens and kills humour. It is an odd reflection that some of the most perceptive, ingenious, 'intellectual' jokes are so conditioned by topical reference that they die within months and are not to be resurrected, even by half a page of exegesis; while others, devoid of all import above the commonplace, survive in their impoverished way from generation to generation. Blessed are the weak, for they shall inherit the mirth.

Of course explications should be unnecessary; if a joke has to be explicated before it can be understood, someone is taking a joke a bit too far. My explications, however, are not intended to explain the joke to the reader. I would hardly wish to seem so patronizing. Their purpose is to link the content of the humour to my perception of its linguistic or stylistic structure – in short, to demonstrate an analysis. This applies particularly to Chapter 3, which addresses itself to the structure of what I call 'locative' or 'formulaic' jokes. Elsewhere in the book I have been less obviously at pains to expound the content of jokes, and it is quite possible that here and there I have left the reader to brood, without benefit of explication, over some opaque pleasantry.

I must add a hope that in style and presentation the text may not seem too irregular; now studious, now breaking into truant fits of clowning. To say that this is my temperament is, in general, no excuse, but I may surely plead in this one instance that my stylistic habit accords with the subject of the book. I can never think that seriousness of purpose is proved by the banishment of laughter; I would a thousand times rather my books were packed with jokes, alive-alive-oh, than jammed with jargon; and I hope I may not be damned for taking a little pleasure by the way; but in case anyone should be exasperated by my periodic surges of frivolity and my occasional impulse to bury the bones of a private pun in the middle of a public paragraph, let me beg an indulgent hearing. As a rule it will be found that the buffoonery substantiates a case.

Writing on so humane a matter, so near to all hearts, I have yet felt curiously isolated, for the want of people who would take my activities in earnest. All the greater, then, is my debt to Ronald Carter, who has understood the issues raised, and who has been unfailing in his sympathy, support, and provocative interest. For his helpful comments during our many discussions he has my warmest thanks. I am greatly indebted to my editor, Randolph Quirk, for his detailed and constructive criticisms, and to my kind and patient publisher, who must sometimes have wondered if the book was worth waiting for. I hope he will think it was. At times, when I have brooded on the question *Who will read all this*?, I have found a dispiriting answer in

Desdemona's conclusion, *Nobody; I myself; farewell.* Yet I venture to hope that the book may find acceptance among those who are interested in the use of language and in the study of comic style.

University of Nottingham WN

NOTE

Unless otherwise documented, literary extracts used for the purpose of illustration are followed by a number referring to an item in the bibliography. Where it is deemed necessary, the item number is accompanied by a page or line-number.

Acknowledgements

We are grateful to the following for permission to reproduce copyright material:

Associated Book Publishers Ltd & Pantheon Books Inc (A Division of Random House Inc.) for extract from poem 'Jill' p 18 *Knots* by R. D. Laing, pub. Tavistock Publications. Copyright © 1970 by the R. D. Laing Trust; The Bodley Head Ltd for an extract from 'My Financial Career' in *Literary Lapses* by Stephen Leacock; The Bodley Head, Dodd & Mead & Co Inc. & McClelland & Stewart Ltd for extracts from 'Sorrows of a Supersoul' in *Nonsense Novels* by Stephen Leacock; Andre Deutsch Ltd & Little Brown & Co in Association with The Atlantic Monthly Press for poem 'England Expects' by Ogden Nash from *I Wouldn't have Missed It* (Deutsch 1983) & *I'm a Stranger Here Myself*, Copyright 1936 by The Curtis Publishing Co. First appeared in *The Saturday Evening Post*; authors' agents for extracts from 'Wellcome to the Caves of Arta' in *Poems and Satires* by Robert Graves; G. K. Hall & Co for poem 'Ravins of the Piute Poet Poe' by C. L. Edson from *The Antic Muse*; Michael Joseph Ltd for poem 'Little Jim' by John Farmer in *Parlour Poetry* by Michael P. Turner; Leicester University Press for extracts from poems 'Changed' & 'Gemini and Virgo' by C. S. Calverley in *The English Poems of Charles Stuart Calverley* ed. H. D. Spear, Copyright © L. U. P. 1974; The Marvell Press for poem 'I Remember, I Remember' by Philip Larkin from *The Less Deceived*; G. P. Putnam & Sons for an extract from poem 'The Anatomy of Humour' from *Spilt Milk* by Maurice Bishop, 1942; Random House Inc. for extracts from 'The Practical Joker' by W. S. Gilbert from *Plays and Poems of W. S. Gilbert*; Raglan Squire F.R.I.B.A., M.S.I.A., for an extract from *Collected Parodies* by Sir John Squire, pub. Hodders 1977.

To the dear memory of my mother,
Harriet Nash,
bravest and merriest of souls,
who so often wept with laughter,
and for whom I, laughing,
must always weep.

One

Explaining the joke

Though nothing suffocates humour more swiftly than a thesis, the comic muse will never lack commentators. Sooner or later, protesting our good intentions, acknowledging the futility of the enterprise, we are all drawn to this challenge: explain the joke. The need to explain becomes, indeed, an obsession rooted in our common lot, for as Bergson rightly remarks, *the comic does not exist beyond the pale of what is strictly human*. Together with the power of speech, the mathematical gift, the gripping thumb, the ability to make tools, humour is a specifying characteristic of humanity. For many of us, it is more than an amiable decoration on life; it is a complex piece of equipment for living, a mode of attack and a line of defence, a method of raising questions and criticizing arguments, a protest against the inequality of the struggle to live, a way of atonement and reconciliation, a treaty with all that is wilful, impaired, beyond our power to control.

In short, as wise men often remind us – with a wink of paradox – humour is a serious business, a land for which the explorer must equip himself thoughtfully. Here we find wit and word-play and banter and bumfun; slogans and captions and catchwords; allusion and parody; ironies; satires; here are graffiti and limericks; here is the pert rhyme, and here the twisted pun; here are scrambled spellings and skewed pronunciations; here is filth for the filthy (you and me), and here are delicacies for the delicate (me and you). How extraordinary that such multiplicity should be denoted by a single word! The sheer variety of phenomena is a temptation to the thesis-maker. He must try to explain what it is that makes one pursuit of all joking, from high comedy to the low snigger, and one family of all jokers, from the deft verbal designers of fiction and poetry down to the aerosol masters of back walls and bridge arches.

1.1 STAGES OF EXPLANATION: (A) THE CULTURE OF THE JOKE

Since we are to follow this course, let us begin by trying to point out all that might be involved in the explanation of a fairly obvious joke – assuming that it had to be expounded to some galactic incomer. Here is a piece of anonymous doggerel:

Little Willie from the mirror
  Licked the mercury right off,
Thinking, in his childish error,
  It would cure the whooping cough.
At the funeral, his mother
  Smartly quipped to Mrs Brown:
'Twas a chilly day for Willie
When the mercury went down!

Not everyone finds this amusing; foreign students are often either puzzled or embarrassed by its complacent callousness ('but such a *mother*!'), and some native speakers are bored by whimsy. What is important, however, is to recognize and accept the *intention* to joke; from that recognition we can proceed through explanatory stages that takes us from the cultural history of the specimen down to its actual wording.

In the first place, this story of Little Willie is not an anecdote without antecedents. It has a derivation, in the facts of child mortality in Victorian/Edwardian times, and in the consequent existence of dozens of poems and pathetic ballads about dying children. Little Willie (whose name was mockingly conferred, by the rude British soldiery, on Crown Prince Wilhelm of Germany) is one of the most persistently versified figures of late-nineteenth-century popular literature:

Poor little Willie
  With his many pretty wiles;
Worlds of wisdom in his look
  And quaint, quiet smiles;
Hair of amber, touched with
  Gold of Heaven so brave,
All lying darkly hid
  In a workhouse grave. [31]

Though the name of Little Willie tops the pathetic polls, it is rivalled in song and story by those of other mortally afflicted cherubs – for example, Little Jim, who figures in an affecting dialogue with his grief-stricken mother:

> She gets her answer from the child,
> Soft fell these words from him –
> 'Mother, the angels do so smile
> And beckon Little Jim.
>
> I have no pain, dear mother, now,
> But oh! I am so dry;
> Just moisten poor Jim's lips again,
> And, mother, don't you cry.'
>
> With gentle, trembling haste she held
> The tea-cup to his lips;
> He smiled to thank her, as he took
> Three tiny little sips. [31]

In course of time, his pathos lapsed, Jim the virtuous babe became an object for ruthless parody:

> 'I have no pain, dear mother, now,
> But oh! I am so dry:
> Connect me to a brewery
> And leave me there to die.' [31]

That poignant stanza brings us back to our original example, because it is a corroborative illustration of the development of a certain kind of humour. Between the Victorian parlour-recitations and the grim social and personal realities they reflect, there is, we may say, an affective association. They not only treat the theme of child mortality seriously and sympathetically; they also have the psychological functions of propitiating grief by paying tribute to it, generalizing the individual sorrow, providing postures of acceptance. With the mocking parody comes a *dissociation*, an apparent reneging of the emotions. The worthy feeling lapses, is withdrawn at the very moment when it should be at its strongest. Why is this? Is it really because the parodist has hardened his heart against these wretched infants and their lachrymose parents, and wants to hold them up to cruel ridicule? Hardly. His target, surely, is not the social *fact*, but the literary *form*; and one reason for the dissociation of feeling on which the joke depends could simply be that the facts are altered or mitigated. Suppose that there is a steep decline in the rate of infant mortality – *eg* with the introduction of vaccines; then it becomes possible to make fun of the forms of expression once affectively associated with it. Such an explanation might not apply to all types of 'heartless' or 'black' humour; but it seems plausible in the present instance.

1.2 STAGES OF EXPLANATION: (B) MATERIAL FACTS

Humour nearly always supposes some piece of factual knowledge shared by humorist and audience. It may be a matter of common historical information – *eg* that Henry VIII had six wives, or that Nelson had one eye, or that Lincoln was assassinated in a theatre. (*But apart from that, Mrs Lincoln, how did you enjoy the show*?) More often, however, it is simply a question of domestic acquaintance with the world and the ordinary substance of living – knowing, say, that Coventry is a place in the English midlands, knowing that in most British towns the buses are double deckers, knowing that the Pope presides over a city called the Vatican, perhaps also knowing that there exists a whisky called *Vat* 69 (whence the ancient and child-charming joke that *Vat* 69 is the Pope's telephone number). To understand the broadest humour one must be broadly informed, not with the stuff of scholarship but with things that one ought to know before being allowed to board the Clapham omnibus.

The rhymester of Little Willie presupposes that we are acquainted with the use of mercury in silvering the backs of mirrors. He also assumes the knowledge that mercury is used in thermometers; and of course he takes for granted our awareness that this substance is poisonous. Unless these facts are in our heads, the joke goes nowhere. Of course it is possible to explain them fairly quickly, but then they are no longer 'lively' facts; they are possessed distantly, we may say, as one might be studiously apprised of the material allusions underlying an Elizabethan joke. This is foreign to the essentially timekeeping spirit of humour. We seldom laugh at jokes that depend on how things used to be. Humour, rejoicing in the moment, flies with the moment; and if I still smile, as indeed I do, at the 'facts' of Little Willie, it may be that I am dating myself by chuckling at things-as-they-are-no-longer. (Is mercury still used in the manufacture of mirrors? How far has its use in thermometers been overtaken by that of coloured alcohol?)

1.3 STAGES OF EXPLANATION: (C) LOGIC AND LIKELIHOOD

Jokers are in the habit of putting up circus-hoops through which their clients must obligingly leap, to achieve the reward of laughter. The hoops are called 'does this follow?' and 'is this likely?', and as we pass swiftly through them we obediently discard our notions of logic and likelihood. It may seem undignified to allow the ringmaster-humorist to make fools of us in this way; but really, the assent we give to the absurdities of a joke is no more contemptible than the licence we allow to the inventions of a fairy story. In the transaction of any tall tale, there is an *executant*, who fixes the rules, and a *respondent*, who accepts the conditions offered, and paradoxically allows himself to be duped in order to enjoy the superiority of his insight. A joke can be a perverse experience, psychologically; the understanding is degraded so that it may rise again.

In the tale of Little Willie, certain unlikely assumptions are enjoined upon us. The major breach of likelihood is that a mother would want to joke about the death of her child, particularly at the funeral; that is, in effect, the hoop through which our minds must boldly jump. But while we balk at that, or giggle at our own daring in making the leap, we forget that we have already cleared another obstacle, hardly less preposterous – namely that a very young child, ravaged by whooping cough, would (a) reason with himself about a cure for his condition, and (b) consequently arrive at a decision to lick the back of his mirror. (The phrase *in his childish error* works cunning wonders in setting up this part of the joke.) Of course this is absurd. An infant does not observe his own symptoms and prescribe a cure for the disease. As for Willie's solution to his woes, it is surely a remarkable case of what Piaget calls 'concrete operational thinking' – in other words, suck-it-and-see. He is precociously gifted with unavailing powers of mind – or so we must believe; for unless we accept that, we lose the jest. This is no clumsy misadventure. This is the tragedy of the infant philosopher who tackles the problem and gets the wrong answer.

1.4 STAGES OF EXPLANATION: (D) THE DIRECTIVE OF FORM

Jokes are often announced, sometimes with a crude forewarning signal (*Have you heard this one*?; *That reminds me . . .*; *A funny thing happened . . .*), sometimes more subtly, through the actual form in which they are presented. The listener or reader recognizes a convention, realizes that he has met something like this before, understands that his wits are being keyed and preconditioned to the acceptance of humour. If, for example, I hear the statement *There was an old lady of Slough*, the odds are that I will register the onset of a limerick, and the limerick is an exclusively humorous form; I will therefore prepare to be amused, and may be mildly surprised, to say the least of it, if this opening clause turns out to be the preliminary to a serious narrative. This aspect of the subject calls for some further exploration, but for the moment let us note the importance of signalling the *intention* to joke. Its importance is in sanctioning laughter, in helping to overcome any scruples or reservations we might have. (It also prompts us to put on the social smile when the joke eludes us.) If the intention to joke is not clearly signalled, making a sort of contract between executant and respondent, laughter is compromised. We have all had the experience of sensing humour in something heard or read, yet not being quite sure whether laughter would be a respectable act or a confession of our own moral deformities. The doubt exists, as often as not, because the humorous intention has not been formally announced.

In the case of the doggerel poem with which all these speculations began, much of the doubt is dispelled by a form that immediately suggests parody of naive folk-metres:

> Little Willie from the mirror
>   Licked the mercury right off,
> Thinking, in his childish error,
>   It would cure the whooping cough.
> At the funeral, his mother
>   Smartly quipped to Mrs Brown:
> 'Twas a chilly day for Willie
>   When the mercury went down!'

We would miss a signal here if we were uncertain about the distinction, in English, between serious verse and doggerel. For the native reader there should be no such difficulty (though indeed we might all find ourselves in difficulties were we to attempt to draw significant lines of definition). Recalling other examples of doggerel, he recognizes characteristic signs in the tick-tock metre (eight tripping syllables followed by seven in each distich) and in the banal rhymes (*off – cough*, *chilly–Willie*). With that recognition comes the understanding that the dreadful message is not to be taken seriously. We may laugh if we wish; the playful form exempts us from paying our dues to the awful reality.

1.5 STAGES OF EXPLANATION: (E) LANGUAGE

Through form we come to language, the trigger that detonates the humorous mass. About its functions, two things may be noted at this point. One is, that there is usually a centre of energy, some word or phrase in which the whole matter of the joke is fused, and from which its powers radiate; and the other is, that the language of humour dances most often on the points of some dual principle, an ambiguity, a figure and ground, an overt appearance and a covert reality. Thus, the hoary old riddle, *What's a Greek urn? – About 100 drachmas a week*, has its humorous centre in the word *urn*, punning with *earn*. (Note, however, that the pun is prepared by another ambiguity; the *'s* of *What's*, the contracted form of *is*, is interpreted as the contraction of *does*.)

These characteristics, of 'pointedness' and 'two-sidedness', also appear in the rhyme of Little Willie. The concentration of linguistic energy is in the final couplet (the *locus* of a joke, to use a term we shall presently adopt, quite often occurs towards the end of its structure), and the trick lies in the management of a carefully prepared ambiguity. The vital element is in the closing phrase, *went down*. A native speaker is of course aware of two meanings here, *ie*: *go down* = 'sink in level' and *go down* = 'be swallowed'. These meanings are related to the dual character of *mercury* in the rhyme, as the measure of temperature and as the poisonous mirror-backing. The duality reflects onto another word, *chilly*, which, thanks to the structuring of the joke, has parallel associations, on the one hand with death ('deathly chill', 'Death lays his icy hand on kings', etc) and on the other with mere temperature ('chilly room', 'chilly journey', etc). The pattern of word-play is presented diagrammatically on *p* 8.

This pattern is introduced by another verbal event, a sort of 'pre-

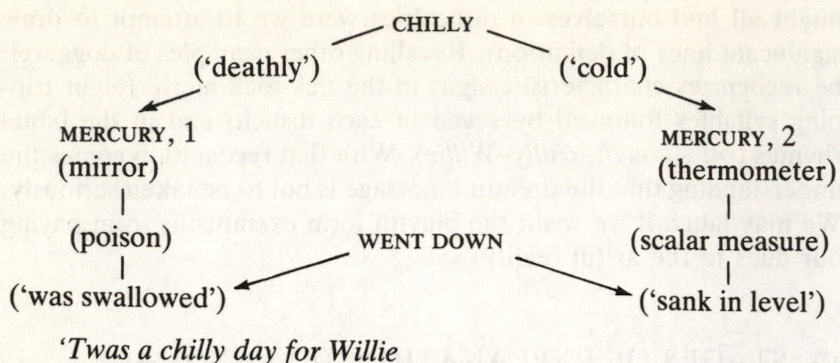

'Twas a chilly day for Willie
When the mercury went down.'

location' whose textual role is equivalent to the comedian's *Here's the punch line*, or *Wait for it, wait for it* – formulae that give ponderous warning of an approaching joke. In the present instance, however, the warning formula – as represented by the phrase *smartly quipped* – is charged with humour. The adverb *smartly* draws together lines of meaning expressed by *wittily*, *humorously*; *perceptively*, *intelligently*; *quickly*, *promptly*; *incisively*, *sharply*.

This vital word is *multivalent*, with components suggesting humour, intelligence, promptitude and incisiveness; and while any of these senses might characterize the joke that follows, none is appropriate to the conventional attitude of a grieving mother. Similar observations might be made about *quipped*; for *quip* connotes humour (possibly sarcastic or biting humour), brevity (or speed of reaction), and word-play. The 'valencies' thus run through the adverb-verb construction, linking its component words. The resultant phrase on the one hand introduces and aptly characterizes the play

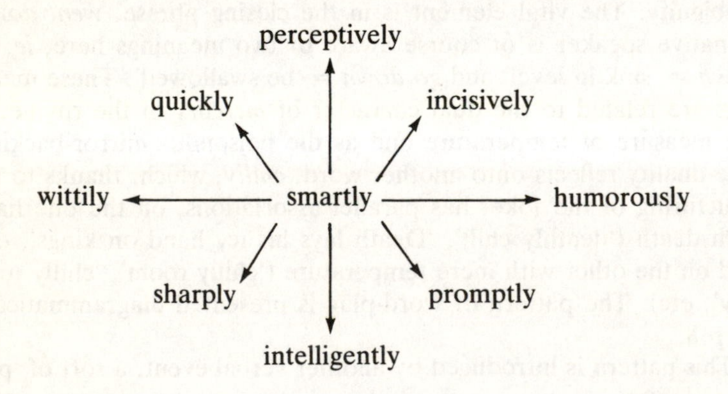

of the final couplet – which is amusing, concise, clever and sardonic – and on the other hand casts the antonymic shadow of constructions like *softly sighed*, *sadly moaned*, which would have the 'right' values if the content of the verse were being taken seriously. (When Little Jim is about to speak, we are told *Soft fell these words from him.*) Here is yet another duality. What is said in jest is stalked by the ghost of what might be conventionally said in earnest:

EARNEST: 'softly sighed' . . . 'it was a terrible moment'

JEST: 'smartly quipped' . . . 'Twas a chilly day for Willie', etc

In short, the linguistic power of the Little Willie joke is contained in the final couplet, where we can discover some features of humorous language that will bear further examination: the location of 'charged' elements at carefully-arranged points in a structure (what comedians call 'timing'), and the play with various dualities, *eg* ambiguity, polysemy, statement and implication. Before this power can be realized, however – before the joke can be discharged in all its swiftness – there is much to be apprehended about cultural and social facts, about shared beliefs and attitudes, about the pragmatic bases of communication. If that sounds laboured and obscure, let us try to put it another way. Humour is not for babes, Martians, or congenital idiots. We share our humour with those who have shared our history and who understand our way of interpreting experience. There is a fund of common knowledge and recollection, upon which all jokes draw with instantaneous effect; though indeed to describe the resources of the fund must seem like an undertaking of tedious length.

1.6 A THESIS TO BEGIN WITH

From all this, something useful and disposable emerges; a thesis to begin with. What it proposes, in brief, is that the 'act' of humour has three principal references:

(a) A 'genus', or derivation, in culture, institutions, attitudes, beliefs, typical practices, characteristic artefacts, etc (whence, in subsequent discussion, the adjective 'generic').

(b) A characteristic design, presentation, or verbal packaging, by virtue of which the humorous intention is indicated and recognized.

(c) A locus in language, some word or phrase that is indispensable to the joke; the point at which humour is held and discharged (whence, as a descriptive term, 'locative').

These references make a general base for more elaborate illustration in later chapters. They invite, however, some preliminary comment.

The generic reference, firstly, is very broad. It includes the social and historical facts which most of us can be assumed to know, the customary patterns of behaviour, the dominant or traditional attitudes, prejudices and stereotypes, the conventional themes and theme-related designs of literature and art. From this reservoir we draw, to begin with, our notions of what is funny *per se*:

Contusions are funny, not open wounds,
 And automobiles that go
Crash into trees by the highwayside;
 Industrial accidents, no.

The habit of drink is a hundred per cent,
 But drug addiction is nil.
A nervous breakdown will get no laughs;
 Insanity surely will.

Humour, aloof from the cigarette,
 Inhabits the droll cigar;
The middle-aged are not very funny;
 The young and the old, they are.

So the funniest thing in the world should be
 A grandsire, drunk, insane,
Maimed in a motor accident,
 And enduring moderate pain. [6; p 207]

Morris Bishop is forced to omit one or two firm favourites – provincials, foreigners, mothers-in-law, politicians, homosexuals, clerics – but his sprightly verse-catalogue makes its point. From such notions of the inherently humorous we derive our joke-stereotypes: 'drunk' jokes, 'Irish' jokes, 'asylum' jokes, 'youth versus age' jokes.

Next, there are commonplaces of allusion, on which varied witticisms can be based. The graffito master who propounds the equation *I drink, therefore I am*; *I'm drunk, therefore I was*, invites us to enjoy locatively his word-play and his skewed grammar; but this we cannot do without first recognizing the derivation of his joke in the Cartesian *cogito, ergo sum*, 'I think, therefore I am.' Academic humour is often a game of recognize-the-quote; but there are ordinary, unacademic, man-in-the-street jokes that also rely on textual allusion, *ie* on references to things said or written in political speeches, advertisements, TV shows, etc. The slogan, catchword, or much-quoted remark becomes a model for cleverly-pointed variations. Larger texts offer scope for essays in parody, lampoon, burlesque, etc, and this is yet another aspect of the generic game. Random examples of parodic models might be the Ten Commandments, Shylock's 'Jew' speech, Keats' *Ode to Autumn*, Dickens' *A Christmas Carol*, The Gettysburg Address, Eliot's *The Waste Land*. Often by their sheer monumentality such exemplars of literary language create standards for our language of humour; they are the solid walls on which our irreverent commentaries are scribbled.

Derivations are often blurred or obscure; it may be that no one knows for certain how a particular type of joke began, or how far it has wandered from its social origins. In such cases the *form* of the joke becomes, as it were, its voucher. Who was Kilroy, polytropic hero of so many brief mural histories? A disgruntled, many-times-posted soldier? An engineer (as has been suggested) in a US Navy maintenance yard? It hardly matters. We recognize the verbal pattern of his joke, *Kilroy was here*, and accept it as the ground out of which other jokes can grow. The intention to joke, as we have already seen, can be announced by a form, and there are many 'micro-forms' which invite the respondent to play the jesting game. For example, the 'banana' jokes much loved by British schoolchildren usually have the question-form *What is A and B and C*?, where *A* and *B* are adjectives, while *C* might be another adjective, or a finite verb, or even a clause: *What's yellow and curved and makes a noise when it travels through water*? The second half of the banana joke, the response, generally answers to the formula *A banana + X*, where *X* is some kind of postmodifying phrase or clause; *A banana with an outboard motor*. There is a kind of ritual associated with the joke, a pattern of predictability and a licence for variation, which we shall later observe in connection with many other micro-forms – one-liners, 'question-and-answer' jokes, aphorisms, 'assertion-

and-tag' forms, concentrated essays in humour with well-marked grammatical and stylistic shapes. One feature of such jokes is that they generate many others on the same model (*eg* the *OK* jokes discussed below, in Ch. 4). Another is, that because they imply some sort of social interaction between the parties to a humorous event (*eg* by way of question and answer or assertion and retort) they are often tiny models of much bigger comic structures. A whole story may be an expansion of one or two joke-types; or, in a novel, long tracts of text may result from the stretching, linking, overlapping, etc of some of these minor forms in their narrative mutations.

To study the locus, or linguistic realization, of a joke means bringing to bear methods of definition, distinction, and categorization familiar to students of stylistics. Like any other variety of usage, the language of humour has to draw on the patterns and implications of phonology and graphology, of syntactic structure, of lexical form, of semantic field. We can therefore study it quite conventionally, as other kinds of discourse are studied, at different levels of linguistic organization, and in doing so we may observe how humorous language shares a characteristic of poetic language, in the frequent convergence of stylistic traits; rhyme or alliteration, for example, may sharply contour a striking grammatical structure that houses some form of lexical play.

It is, however, the *language*, not the linguistic analysis, of humour that must be our general concern; because, paradoxically, linguistics in the strictest sense may not comprehend the humorous activity of language. Humour is an occurrence in a social play. It characterizes the interaction of persons in situations in cultures, and our responses to it must be understood in that broad context, whether it makes the sudden demand of wit, or whether it has the more discursive appeal of description and anecdote.

Two

Witty compression, comic expansion

Metaphors that link laughter and explosiveness ('erupt', 'burst out') touch on an interesting paradox: that the energies of humour, like those of a detonation, are both contractive and expansive. The quickfire gag, the punch-line, the dry aphorism, are irresistible because they compress so powerfully, imply so much in a little compass – a phrase, or even a single word. Such compression is a classic element in the technique of humour; 'brevity', we are inevitably reminded, 'is the soul of wit.' On the other hand, when the compressed meanings erupt and laughter bursts out, its waves and echoes persist, and one outbreak is only the signal for the next. The effect of a joke is often to put us in a state of pleasurable instability that welcomes, craves, indeed *courts* the impact of another joke. This is a requisite of comedy, which depends on *expansion*. The character of a Falstaff or a Pickwick is not created in a single sally; and a deftly-turned witticism does not show us Jerome's tourists lost in Hampton Court maze, or Thurber's eccentric family on the Night The Bed Fell. Wit is planted, comedy flowers. Sometimes it flowers amazingly from a single witty seed; sometimes it is a pricking-out of many varieties; sometimes it is wit grafted onto other humorous stock.

2.1 A STUDY IN COMPRESSION: (A) THE TYPE

Consider the case of a witty graffito: *Living in Coventry is like watching a plank warp*. This may be an unjust aspersion on a fine city; it seems, nonetheless, a funny thing to have written in lugubrious complaint on some dull urban wall, and it illustrates, for those of us who are ignorant of the general quality of life in Coventry, something notable about wit. It shows that we are not required to have the *specific* experience to which the witticism refers, but only to grasp a category, to recognize the *kind* of image that is raised.

This 'Coventry' joke has its genesis in traditional attitudes to regional cities and provincial life. In Britain, such attitudes are at least as old as the eighteenth century, and probably older: *From Hell, Hull, and Halifax, good Lord deliver us*, runs the old adage. The seaside resort with a staid elderly population is often the butt of 'dull town' jokes: *Morecambe, a cemetery with buses*; *Harwich for the continent, Frinton for the incontinent*. (Harwich is a seaport, Frinton a resort for the elderly; on the allusiveness of this elegantly malicious trope, see §5.2.). Commonly, however, this type of joke simply suggests that such-and-such a place is tedious and unattractive (*And on the eighth day, God created Birmingham*), or that it is lost in provincial self-absorption (*Titanic struck by iceberg, Aberdeen woman feared drowned*).

2.2 A STUDY IN COMPRESSION: (B) THE FORM

Though these jokes vary somewhat in form, a recurrent pattern is equational (*A = B*), *eg: Edinburgh – a geriatric ward designed by the brothers Adam*. An extension of the pattern is the 'verdictive' definition (see §3.6), expressed syntactically in the Subject-Complement structure, X is Y: *Newcastle is the pits*. Characteristic of the formula is the possibility of free substitution: for *Newcastle* read the name of any town in the neighbourhood of a coal-mining community. Here, then, is a made-up wit-recipe, in which the chief ingredient can be the name of whatever town the joker happens to dislike (even as I correct my draft of this page I hear, from the television set in the next room, an American voice declaring that *Philadelphia is a graveyard with street lighting*); more freely, here is a model for invention, challenging the playful and the observant to devise complements for *Leicester is. . ., Liverpool is . . . etc*. A further stage of wit-working would be to vary the form of the Subject, so that instead of *Leicester, Nottingham, Manchester*, etc, we have non-finite clauses, *eg*: *To work in Leicester, To see Nottingham, Arriving in Manchester, Living in Coventry*. This is the stage of construction exemplified by our graffito, *Living in Coventry is like watching a plank warp*.

2.3 A STUDY IN COMPRESSION: (C) THE LOCUS

Now it is clear that much of the power of the witticism resides in that one word, *warp*. Here, in an intransitive verb, is the locus of the joke (see §1.6), and if we lack the linguistic competence to grasp its multiple implications, the humour of the remark must be greatly enfeebled. (As it would be, for example, if the line read *Living in Coventry is like watching a plank twist.*) Of course, the single word is not the whole joke, and if we 'replay' the sentence, in thoughtful slow motion, we can see how the squeeze of humour begins in advance of that ultimate act of compression. The equation of *living* with *watching* (*ie* with a *static* process) is important. Equally important is the joke-maker's choice of *plank* rather than *wood*, or *timber*, or *board*. The component of 'thickness' in the meaning of *plank* is essential – and with it, perhaps, the contingent, familiar association of 'thickness' and 'stupidity' (as in the common phrase *as thick as two short planks*). The joke is primed, certainly, before it bursts on us; yet still the main charge is in *warp*. In the current edition of Roget, the index-entries for *warp* include the notions of distortion and deformity, under which headings, in the main text, we find, for example, 'contort', 'twist', 'misshape'. The definition in my desk dictionary is 'make or become crooked, change from straight or right or natural state'. Interestingly, neither thesaurus nor dictionary isolates the component of *warp* that is quite indispensable to this joke, namely *slowness*.

2.4 A STUDY IN EXPANSION; (A) THE TEXT

Now let us take the same joke, so wittily compact in its graffito form, and observe it in an expanded variant. Philip Larkin supplies us with a perfect comparison piece in his ironic, sad, funny poem *I Remember, I Remember* (the title of which alludes, of course, to the well-known *I Remember*, by Thomas Hood):

> Coming up England by a different line
> For once, early in the cold new year,
> We stopped, and, watching men with number-plates
> Sprint down the platform to familiar gates,
> 'Why, Coventry!' I exclaimed. 'I was born here.'

I leant far out, and squinnied for a sign
That this was still the town that had been 'mine'
So long, but found I wasn't even clear
Which side was which. From where those cycle-crates
Were standing, had we annually departed

For all those family hols? . . . A whistle went:
Things moved. I sat back, staring at my boots.
'Was that,' my friend smiled, 'where you "have your roots?"'
No, only where my childhood was unspent,
I wanted to retort, just where I started;

By now I've got the whole place clearly charted.
Our garden, first; where I did not invent
Blinding theologies of flowers and fruits,
And wasn't spoken to by an old hat.
And here we have that splendid family

I never ran to when I got depressed,
The boys all biceps and the girls all chest.
Their comic Ford, their farm where I could be
'Really myself'. I'll show you, come to that,
The bracken where I never trembling sat,

Determined to go through with it; where she
Lay back, and 'all became a burning mist.'
And, in those offices, my doggerel
Was not set up in blunt ten-point, nor read
By a distinguished cousin of the Mayor,

Who didn't call and tell my father: *There*
Before us, *if we could but see ahead* –
'You look as if you wished the place in Hell,'
My friend said, 'judging from your face.' 'Oh well,
I suppose it's not the place's fault,' I said.
'Nothing, like something, happens anywhere.' [19]

The closing maxim, like a graffito, implies a world of instances: (*Nothing*, *like something*, *happens anywhere* is a wittily compressed summary of the joke that has its equivalent in *Living in Coventry is like watching a plank warp*. The implications of the joke, however, have already been spelt out in the preceding text; the humour is presented in expansion.

2.5 A STUDY IN EXPANSION: (B) THE ELABORATIVE INSTANCE

The major humorous device, at which Larkin assiduously works, is that of treating a grammatical negative as a logical or empirical positive. This is a common type of 'philosophical' playfulness; Carroll resorts to it in the Alice books, *eg* in Humpty-Dumpty's concept of the *unbirthday present*. Larkin's poem is a humorous expansion of the implied propositions 'an unevent happened' and 'an event unhappened'; hence, *my childhood was unspent*, and all the other negative marks of positive occurrence in an *anywhere* which is *clearly charted*. The joke is elaborated in a series of grouped instances where the recurrent negatives make the principal cohesive thread:

(i) *Our garden . . . where I did not invent / Blinding theologies of flowers and fruits, / And wasn't spoken to by an old hat.*

(ii) *. . . here we have that splendid family / I never ran to when I got depressed, / The boys all biceps and the girls all chest. / Their comic Ford, their farm where I could be / 'Really myself'.*

(iii) *The bracken where I never trembling sat, / Determined to go through with it; where she / Lay back, and 'all became a burning mist'.*

(iv) *. . . in those offices, my doggerel / Was not set up in blunt ten-point, nor read / By a distinguished cousin of the Mayor, / Who didn't call and tell my father . . .*

In each of these groups, it can be seen how one invention leads to another, through the heuristic mechanisms of language; either because the humorous examples are so many beads on a long syntactic string (as in group (iv), for instance), or because of the rub of semantic associations (as in group (i), where the *blinding* theologies connect with the notion of being *spoken to*). We also see how, as the inventive power luxuriates, the major joke is inlaid with minor jokes (*eg* in group (ii), *The boys all biceps and the girls all chest*). What is apparent here, then, is a verbally exuberant flowering of comic ideas.

2.6 A STUDY IN EXPANSION: (C) THE PARODIC ELEMENT

These 'comic ideas', however, are in the main echoic of notions and phrases that we have met before, and Larkin's poem is to a great extent an essay in parody. In some cases, a cliché is explicitly mocked by its inverted commas: 'mine', 'where you have your roots', 'really myself', 'all became a burning mist'. The Mayor's cousin's unspeech is also parodically marked, by the italic type. Other phrases, *eg*: *family hols*, *determined to go through with it*, go unpointed, but any reader with a basic literary competence notes them, and is aware of their 'period' associations with junior magazines and pulp fiction for adolescents. Indeed, all the fun of the piece is at the expense of some threadbare notions (plus the accompanying conventional language) derived from third-rate narrative of the 'confessional' type – the debased *Bildungsroman.* The humour of the piece is enhanced by our recognition that these images *are* fictional, that they *are* the happenings of life re-worked by the imagination. We know that the artist does not look like this young man.

A further element in the parody, and an important one, is its sly allusiveness to Hood's poem. That, too, has its 'elaborative instances' – not of a governing joke, but of a feeling of childhood joy; Hood mentions the house where he was born, the window of his room, the fir trees, the laburnum his brother planted, the various flowers – from which he creates, if not exactly *blinding theologies*, at least a hint of Trahernian beatitude:

> I remember, I remember,
> The roses, red and white,
> The vi'lets and the lily-cups,
> Those flowers made of light!

The poem ends with a sombre reflection. Brooding on his boyish fantasy that the tops of the fir-trees were 'close against the sky', Hood says:

> It was a childish ignorance,
> But now 'tis little joy
> To know I'm farther off from heav'n
> Than when I was a boy.

Larkin's parodic exercise nods wryly towards this neo-romantic picture of childhood as a country close to heaven:

> 'You look as though you wished the place in Hell,'
> My friend said . . .

The traveller rejects the 'friend's' speculation. He is 'farther off from' some experience, certainly, but not a Hell or a Heaven. The something he is 'farther off from' is Nothing. That is the humour of the poem; and its melancholy.

2.7 A STUDY IN EXPANSION: (D) THE RESPONDENT

This 'friend' plays a part in the development of the joke; he is the audience, apparently, the person who might seem, at first glance, to be standing as respondent in the reader's stead. In fact, the plotting of the poem is a little more complicated than that. There are writings that require, *within the text*, an executant and a respondent, whose interchanges are monitored by the respondent-outside-the-text:

$$(E \longrightarrow)\ E_t \longleftrightarrow R_t\ (\longleftarrow R)$$

E = executant: author, poet, wit, original 'I'.

E_t = executant-within-the-text: the *persona* who speaks for the author, perhaps, without necessarily *being* the author.

R_t = respondent-within-the-text: the *persona* controlled by the executant-within-the-text, and making responses shared or disclaimed by the respondent-outside-the-text.

R = respondent: the reader, as observer and censor.

This is the pattern of the Larkin poem. From virtually the first word, '*Why, Coventry*! . . . *I was born here*', to the last '*Nothing, like something*, *happens anywhere*', the poet uses or implies direct speech – which, of course, has to be directed *at* someone. That 'someone' is ultimately the reader; it is really the reader to whom the remark 'I'll show you' is addressed, and to whom the map of

Nothing is revealed. There has to be, however, a friend-in-the-text, to imply observation of all the bearings demonstratively marked in the 'clear charting' of the place: *our garden, that family, their farm, those offices*. There is a half-illusion that these things can actually be seen from the train. Part of the complex literary joke is that the tale of elaborative instances is not actually recited to the 'friend', the respondent-within-the-text. It is received in privileged communication by the reader, the respondent-outside. The outsider is admitted to the game; the 'friend', the insider, is excluded. This is an example of intricate textual planning, a strategy different in quality and consequence from what happens when 'I' tell 'you' a joke.

2.8 ORAL AND TEXTUAL HUMOUR

This brings us to a matter of some importance, *ie* the styles of oral and textual humour. Between these styles, apart from the obvious contrast of speaking/listening versus writing/reading, there are important technical differences. One difference, of direct concern, is that textual humour expands through elaborative networks rarely if ever found in oral humour. When oral humour is expanded, its commonest course is the repetition of a joke-type, or the assiduous 'working' of some evident situation or theme. A company of friends may fall to punning, and will try to out-pun each other in variants of increasing extravagance; two children will make rival exchanges of 'elephant' jokes or 'banana' jokes; a club comedian, judging the mood of his audience, will produce a run of jokes on some clearly favoured theme – domestic relationships, shall we say, or current political events. (In connection with this, a colleague, citing the troubles in Northern Ireland, has suggested that oral humour both expresses, and is used to relieve, psychic tensions; so that the worse the Northern Irish situation, the greater the number of 'Irish' jokes.) In the expansions of oral humour there is often an element of competitiveness, of opportunism, of response to the immediate and emergent situation.

Textual humour expands in ways more subtle and comprehensive, sustaining itself through devices that converge and react upon each other. What begins as a game, on the bounce of a lucky notion or the teasing flight of a word, ends as an art, with diverse elements wrought together in a scrupulous design. There is of course the limitation of all texts, that the design is made once and for all, without possibility of an adaptive improvisation, for the distant, anonymous respondent who must interpret complex signals made via the restrictive conventions of print. There is also, however, the corresponding strength of all texts, the strength of a permanent record that can store, for later recovery, the details of a complicated narrative pattern.

2.9 MODES OF EXPANSION

It is largely through the study of texts, then, that we are able to observe the modes of humorous expansion. Three types emerge, identifiable as *generic*, *linguistic*, and *interactional*. *Generic* refers to such elements as are discussed in §1.6 – elements of a 'genus' or *genre*, not only of literary forms and conventions, but also of cultural facts. *Linguistic* obviously alludes to the patternings of syntax, semantics, and sound, while *interactional* stands for the relationship of executant and respondent (comedian/audience, writer/reader, Character A/Character B) and the suppositions and entailments that are the pragmatic or logical basis of their relationship. The features principally expressing these modes of expansion may be briefly summarized:

Expansion is:

(a) Generic in: allusion to facts, social conventions and traditions, culture, literary works

parodies of styles (individual styles, period styles, styles of specific works) or parodies of social conventions and attitudes

the interplay of form and content (or the conventional matching of certain kinds of structure with certain kinds of significance; eg: the use of the epistolary or diary form as a vehicle for humorous monologue)

(b) Interactional in: the pragmatics of response – eg: the writer's control of his reader; the signalling of an intention to joke; the predictability or otherwise of reactions the logic of what is proposed; its requirement on the reader to make certain suppositions; its implications, if accepted at face value

(c) Linguistic in: structural mimesis – eg: the recurrence and variation of joke-bearing syntactic structures

coupling mechanisms – eg: features such as rhyme, rhythm, and alliteration, or pointed antitheses ('the boys all biceps and the girls all chest')

semantic concords and dissonances – eg: in synonymy, hyponymy, and antonymy, or in 'normal' and 'deviant' collocations.

Some of these notes may raise questions for later elucidation; it is worth adding here that subsequent chapters will correspond to the progression from 'generic' (Ch. 3–5), to 'interactional' (Ch. 6) to 'linguistic' (Ch. 7–8).

2.10 THE COMPRESSIVE WITHIN THE EXPANSIVE

Many passages of expansive comedy are packed with witty compressions; the two aspects of humour are certainly not mutually exclusive. Here, for example, are a few lines from the opening page of Evelyn Waugh's *Decline and Fall*:

> For two days they had been pouring into Oxford;
> epileptic royalty from their villas of exile; uncouth
> peers from crumbling country seats; smooth young men
> of uncertain tastes from embassies and legations;
> illiterate lairds from wet granite hovels in the
> Highlands; ambitious young barristers and Conservative
> candidates torn from the London season and the indelicate
> advances of debutantes; all that was most sonorous of
> name and title was there for the beano [33]

The *beano* is the 'annual dinner of the Bollinger club', at which champagne, in large quantities, is uproariously consumed; so that the final word of our passage (and, incidentally, of Waugh's paragraph) is the locus of a joke. For a champagne supper, *beano* has all the wrong – therefore comically *right* – connotations.

That one word, then, is powerfully compressive. The humorous impact of the passage, on the other hand, does not depend on the locative strength of single words. The important stylistic unit is the noun phrase, *eg*: *illiterate lairds from wet granite hovels in the Highlands*. In this example, it appears that the humour is densely crammed into every part of the construction. Every word, apart from prepositions and the definite article, makes a contribution to the joke, and it would not be possible to cancel or change anything without impairing the comic power of the phrase. There is a chain of humorous elements linked partly by alliteration ('*ill*iterate *l*airds', '*h*ovels in the *H*ighlands'), partly by sharp dissonances of meaning in the adjective-noun collocations (*lairds* are surprisingly *illiterate*, *hovels* are unexpectedly *granite*). Within this construction, then, humour expands linguistically through two convergent devices: alliterative coupling and semantic contrast.

But our chosen example is only one among several carefully-graded instances. A tabulation of successive noun phrases will show (a) how the basic structure of *premodifier – head – postmodifier* is repeated, and (b) how the repetitions vary and extend the form, sometimes by extending the premodifying sequence, sometimes by amplifying the head, but chiefly by elaborating the post-modifying pattern:

PREMODIFIERS	HEAD		POSTMODIFIERS
epileptic	royalty		from their villas of exile
uncouth	peers		from crumbling country seats
smooth young	men	of uncertain tastes	from embassies and legations
illiterate	lairds		from wet granite hovels in the Highlands
ambitious young	barristers and Conservative candidates		torn from the London season and the indelicate advances of debutantes

The stylistic importance, in the passage, of syntactic imitation and syntactic variation appears clearly from this table. The right-hand column in particular shows the mimetic outgrowth of a syntactic type, the prepositional construction (*ie: 'from X'*) which plays some variations on the noun phrase (*villas of exile, crumbling country seats, embassies and legations, wet granite hovels in the Highlands*) before merging into another syntactic type, the participle clause consisting of a verb, *torn*, and an adverbial adjunct headed by *from*. This final instance not only gives locative emphasis to *torn* (not 'coaxed', 'tempted', 'enticed', *etc*, but *torn*, as in 'wrested', 'wrung', 'wrenched'); it also creates, in its expansiveness, a joke-within-the-joke, about a new set of personae, the debutantes. Here the generic and the linguistic expansion coincide; the reader is expected to know about a genus of social conventions – *ie* what the London season was, why ambitious young Conservatives might be so interested in it as to have to be *torn* from it, what debutantes were, and why they should have found it necessary to make advances (indelicate ones at that) to ambitious young men. Generically, as linguistically, this is the crown of a joke that has risen through several stages.

Two linguistic devices imprint the passage: alliteration, a coupling device, and dissonant collocation, a contrastive device. We have pointed out in one example the stylistic trick that is played repeatedly in phonological couplings (*e*pileptic, *e*xile; un*c*outh, *c*rumbling, *c*ountry; *s*mooth, un*c*ertain; i*ll*iterate, *l*airds; *h*ovels, *H*ighlands) and in the incongruous attributions (*epileptic royalty, uncouth peers, crumbling country seats, illiterate lairds, wet granite hovels*) where for the most part a pejorative attribute attaches to a 'dignified' noun, though in one instance (*granite hovels*) it is the noun that 'disgraces' its epithet. Not every joke in the passage is created in this way, however. There are one or two witticisms of unique structure, *eg*: *smooth young men of uncertain tastes*. The locus of this is in the postmodifier *of uncertain tastes*, and the linguistic point lies in a lexical/semantic distinction between *taste* (= connoisseurship, cultivation, *etc*) and *tastes* (= preferences, predilections, fancies). The expressions *man of uncertain taste* and *man of uncertain tastes* do not amount to quite the same thing; the distinction, moreover, affects the meaning of the adjective *uncertain*, which in the one case is roughly synonymous with 'unformed', 'erratic', 'unsystematic', and in the other with 'dubious', 'questionable', 'controversial', 'perverse'.

The expansion of humour in this text somewhat resembles the commonplace expansion of oral humour, in that a joke-formula (*adjective*-SOMEBODY-*from*, *etc*) is repeated and varied. It is unlike oral humour, though, in the elaboration – the *networking* – of its comic outgrowth. In successive formulae, the joking is *multilocative*; there is more than one place where we are invited to laugh, and where much humour would be lost if a word were cancelled. With the variations on the formula, jokes bud on jokes; thus *epileptic royalty from their villas of exile* is the basic construction, but with *smooth young men of uncertain tastes from legations and embassies*, something new is added to the formulaic routine. Furthermore, the sequence of jokes in the passage has a cohesion which is both generic, in its allusions to the fashionable society of the 1920s, and linguistic in its deliberate play with the conjoint principles of phonetic consonance and semantic dissonance. All this illustrates very well the phrase we have coined to describe the expansion of textual humour: *diverse elements wrought together in a scrupulous design*. So we might characterize the language of comedy at large; yet the same characteristics of patterning, of careful arrangement, of well-timed emphasis, of generic complexity, may indeed be discerned in the common joke, the epigram, the slogan, the muralled wisecrack, the most trivial component of the humorist's craft.

Three

The design of the joke: (i) locative formulae

3.1 A DIGRESSION ON NARRATIVE

Look. Out of the distance, over the baked and burnished plain, along the rattlesnake trail that winds past red, uprearing buttes, comes the stagecoach. And here, in the foreground, behind a rock that tops a rise, we see a group of men. Who they are, we do not know. We do know, from their stubbled faces, their greasy waistcoats, their crushed and begrimed headgear, that they are up to no good. Their very horses are mud-coloured and nameless. It is a matter of certain prediction that when the coach draws abreast of the rock, these men will rob it. We do not yet know how the robbery will proceed – whether a boulder will roll downhill into the path of the horses, whether a shot will tumble the guard from his perch, or whether, after a prolonged chase, the most athletic bandit will swing on the harness between the lead horses and bring the equipage to a standstill. What we are assured of is, that given these elements – the coach in the distance, the men lurking behind the rock – the narrative must take a certain turn; elements of structure enable us to predict a course of events.

But stay – even while the malefactors are taking aim – who is this, riding towards us from yonder town of Tombstone? His waistcoat has been drycleaned, and his comely hat, neatly blocked and brushed, sits agreeably atop his bronzed, regular, firm, scrupulously-razored features. He is dazzlingly dentifriced, and his horse, wash-day-white, answers to the name of Flash. On his newly-laundered shirt is pinned a conspicuous star. Of a certainty, this is the sheriff, and his arrival is going to change matters. We must now reconsider our position. The stage will not, after all, be robbed. Hearing gunfire, the keen executive of the law will spur his mount ('*Hi-yuh, Flash*!') towards the provocative noise; the desperadoes will be outgunned and outwitted; one or two will die spectacular deaths and the rest will be driven off; the stage will get through.

Will get through, that is, if and only if the sheriff is drawn towards those crackerjack pistols and the periodic boom of the guardian shotgun. But what now? See – our man rides head-heavy, preoccupied, seemingly heedless of the fusillade. What is amiss? Listen – he mutters to himself: '*Danged ef thuh goldurned batt'ries in mah hayrin'-aid ain't plumb tuckered out agin.*' Can such things be? *A deaf sheriff*!? Why, what becomes of our predictions now? Narrative ingenuity is baffled by this perverse circumstance.

A problem indeed – but here comes another, for the leader of the bandits has removed his battered black Stetson to reveal a discreet skull-cap – yes, truly, a *yarmulka*. A pious Jew of good family, for all his despicable trade, he has just learned to his consternation that by a mistaken reckoning (last year's calendar – a ludicrously false economy) they have set out to rob the stage on a *Saturday*. In every fibre of his Jewish being he is appalled. '*On the Sabbath you want I should rob the stage? I should plunder and ravage, God forbid, like it was Tuesday already?*' Chastened, his companions holster their guns, and prepare to withdraw. This is a momentous shift in the structural balance, cancelling the sheriff, indeed cancelling everything, for now there will be no robbery, no gunfight, and the stage will rattle ignorantly down the winding trail to Tombstone. Between them, Dan the Deaf Sheriff and Benjamin the Orthodox Bushwhacker have managed to confound all prediction. So –

Question: *Where do we go from here?*
Answer: *We get on to the next stage.*

3.2 TWO ASPECTS OF JOKE DESIGN: (A) THE NARRATIVE SHAPE

For the foregoing frivolity, with its excruciating final pun (puns are conventionally 'excruciating') we may plead a double excuse. Firstly, it makes a bridge from the discussion of 'compression' and 'expansion' in Chapter 2; here is an expanded narrative, ending in the compression of a wisecrack. Secondly, and consequently, it introduces the proposition that there are two aspects of joke design, one having to do with the method of extended narration, the other with the construction of witticisms in formulaic patterns.

The stagecoach story mocks some of the time-honoured conventions of the 'Western' film. (This is the basis of its *generic reference* – for which term, see § 1.6.) Narrative predictions are frustrated, and the tale apparently collapses into rigmarole shapelessness, as though the essential inner frame of counterpoised elements had been knocked away. In fact, it is symmetrically constructed; what has been removed is the possibility of a convincing moment of asymmetry, and with it such an outcome as we are accustomed to in many simple tales.

This no doubt requires elaboration. Consider, then, a possible

Phase	Action A		Action B
I	stagecoach approaches	→	bandits lurk behind large boulder
			↓
	stagecoach party defend themselves	←	bandits leap out and attack stagecoach
II	sheriff appears	→	bandits take cover behind smaller boulders
			↓
	sheriff skilfully exploits rocks, dead trees, humps, tussocks, declivities, etc.	←	bandits try to shoot sheriff
III	sheriff and stagecoach party coordinate their efforts in a counter-attack on the bandits	→	bandits at first resist but their leader is killed
			↓
			bandits surrender, and are arrested by the sheriff.

structure for a story to be called *Robbing the Stage*. It is built up in phases, as illustrated on *p.* 28; the arrows indicate the progression of the narrative:

Phases I and II are symmetrically constructed, each move being matched by a counter-move. Phase III, however, is asymmetrical; here we posit the move that has no counter or consequence, and is therefore the concluding act, the terminal statement, the 'outcome'. Most simple narratives are constructed so as to lead, in this way, to an issue; many, but not all, comic tales have this form.

Contrast this with the story related in I above. This begins with a symmetry of action:

stagecoach approaches —— bandits lurk behind large boulder

but does not then alternate the moves from phase to phase until a point of asymmetry is reached. Instead, it substitutes for the action-symmetry a pattern of symmetrically matching attributes. These, furthermore, are of two kinds: 'generic' attributes (*ie* those observed in 'Western' film convention) and caricature attributes devised by the humorist. The structure may be summarized thus:

Action counterpoise:	stagecoach approaches	vs	bandits lurk behind boulders
Attribute counterpoise: (a) 'generic'	sheriff in clean clothes on a named horse	vs	bandits in dirty clothes, with nameless horses
Attributes counterpoise: (b) caricature	sheriff is deaf	vs	bandit leader is Jewish

From this descriptive stasis no outcome is possible, but still the piece has a design: a design consisting of attributive matchings rather than of counterpoised actions. Thus it mocks the commonplace progression of rudimentary narratives, in which, *things happening as they do*, an ending appears; here, *things being what they are*, no conclusion offers itself. It is a different kind of design, no less legitimate or effective than the other; some comic narratives take this form, perhaps because, in its deadlock of absurdities, it suggests the pattern of life itself.

3.3 TWO ASPECTS OF JOKE DESIGN: (B) THE LOCATIVE WITTICISM

Onto the end of our narrative, to provide a sort of conclusion, we have tacked a mild witticism:

> *Question*: 'Where do we go from here?'
> *Answer*: 'We get on to the next stage.'

This illustrates a second aspect of joke design. With the foregoing narrative in mind, the reader is primed to understand this commentary joke, and sees that its locus is in the phrase *the next stage*; since *stage* = (1) 'stagecoach', and (2) 'phase in a process, exposition, etc'. He must also be aware of the 'pre-locative' design (on 'prelocation, see §1.5). If *stage* is punningly used, *get on to* is a pun-in-advance, or preparatory twist, involving the meanings (1) 'board', and (2) 'proceed to or towards'. This pun is in its turn anticipated by the verb *go* in the opening question; *go* may = (1) 'physical movement', or (2) 'mental progression'.

Thus a meaning is derived from the stagecoach story, and is presented as a punning response. The response might conceivably be paraphrased in the form:

> Well, we have failed to tell a conclusive story. Let us start again and see if we can manage more convincingly next time.

This is a maker's wry assessment of his work. Then again, we might summarize the joking message thus:

> So much for illustrative material. Now let us explore the theoretical issues it raises.

This is an expositor's impudent justification of his procedures. Or we might even consider it possible to bear both interpretations in mind (plus any others that may offer themselves), and regard the joke as a case of academic skittishness. It is, to be sure, a fairly feeble witticism, such strength as it has being located in the word *stage*.

3.4 STRUCTURAL RELATIONSHIPS

This question-and-answer joke is constructed upon the basis of the stagecoach rigmarole; it is simply not possible to see it as a joke, or respond to its punning language, without being acquainted with the underlying narrative. Similar statements might be made, however, about any manifestation of verbal humour. All jokes that use language are (obviously, one might say) superstructures with some underlay of reference which the reader/listener needs to have in his grasp. In oral humour there is usually a simple relationship between the formulaic superstructure of the joke and a substructure of generic detail. Take, for example, the case of this political graffito: *Guy Fawkes, where are you now that we need you*? The words are to be interpreted with reference to historical and cultural facts, some of which *must* be understood, while others are mere additives, 'flavouring' the joke to individual taste:

SUPERSTRUCTURE (FORMULA)

'Guy Fawkes, where are you now that we need you?'

SUBSTRUCTURE (GENERIC DETAIL)

- In 1605, Guy Fawkes and his associates plotted to blow up Parliament while the House was in session – the so-called Gunpowder Plot.
- In 1981 the Conservative government was not universally popular.

Footnote: There are comparable imprecations (*eg* Wordsworth's 'Milton! Thou shouldst be living at this hour / England hath need of thee. . .'*etc*).

The primary meaning of this joke – in accordance with the starred items – is that in the view of the graffitist Parliament was doing such a bad job that it deserved to be blown up by some spirited subversive. The joke is incidentally tinged by the possibility of reference to other utterances with a similar form, *eg* the opening lines of Wordsworth's sonnet. Wordsworth called on Milton to return and cure, by moral force, the ills of England in 1802; the graffitist calls on Fawkes to reverse the errors of the 1980s with the corrective power of high explosive. And if we seek a further twist in the allusiveness of the jokes, there is a fact not listed above in our schematic layout: the fact that Guy Fawkes failed in his original attempt.

Here we see the relationship that most commonly operates when jokes are told and laughter is raised. The listener/reader has spontaneous resort to his 'generic' knowledge for the particles of information that make sense of the verbal superstructure. The quicker the substructured response to the verbal stimulus, the greater the likelihood of laughter; we are not tickled or prodded into mirth when we must scan the understanding like an encyclopaedia – though it is possible to relish the joke in meditative retrospect by discovering more items in the substructure.

This, however, is a fairly simple account of the structure of humour, assuming that the superstructure is some kind of formula, and that the substructure consists of a few relevant generic details. Such a description would not quite cover the essay in humour which opens this chapter, where an *anecdote*, provides the basis of reference for a *formula*, anecdote and formula sharing a 'generic' substructure, thus:

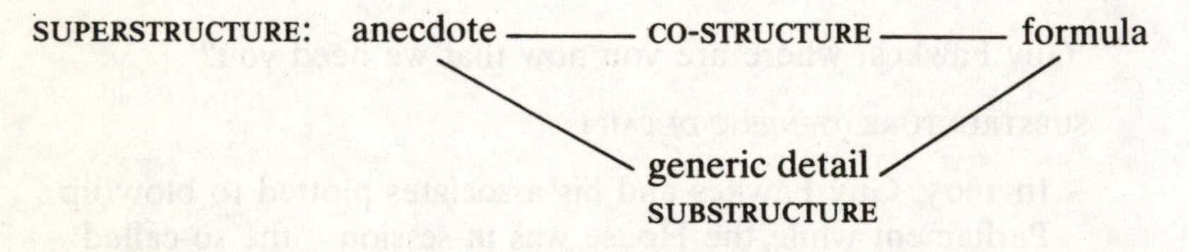

The stagecoach story and its offspring quip are *co-structured*, so that the formula is interpreted with reference to its companion joke, and *substructured* by common allusion to iconographic detail in a popular art-form.

This more sophisticated representation of joke design still does not account for all structural relationships. What are we to say, for example, about the humorous episodes, anecdotal in character, that make up the fabric of many comic texts? All anecdotes have a generic substructure, clearly; but in many cases they also bear reference to another kind of underlying pattern, the design of the continuous narrative. Anecdotal episodes in fiction are often paradigms of a total theme. Not only is it difficult to interpret them fully, as anecdotes, without having access to the underlying narrative design; it is also the case that they are comments on the narrative, illustrating a character, pointing to a motive, often providing the reader with landmarks in the discursive terrain. They may refer, in fact, to a planned discursive substructure, for which a convenient label might be *infrastructure*. A complex piece of humour involves diverse relationships between what is overt – *ie* the text – and what is covert – *ie* the generic detail and the narrative concept:

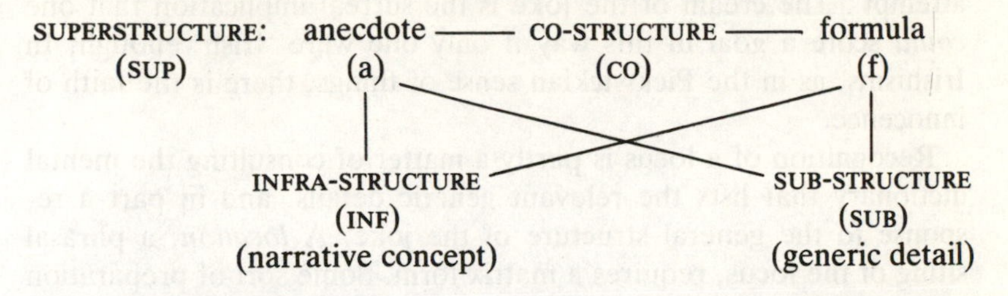

Of the lines of relationship sketched here, two – expressible as *a*/SUB and *f*/SUB – are indispensable; there is a generic content in any joke. The three others, *a*/CO/*f*, *a*/INF, and *f*/INF, are potential constructions. One of them, the relationship of a mere formula to an extensive infrastructure (*f*/INF) is perhaps difficult to envisage, but the first chapter of *Pickwick Papers* affords an example. When Mr Pickwick and a member of his club hotly exchange offensive terms (the hottest is *humbug*), an avenue of escape from the implication of real insult is provided by the assurance that the antagonists are using words *in a Pickwickian sense*, *ie* without their conventional meanings OR with whatever meaning the addressee may choose to assign to them. The joke encapsulated by the phrase *in a Pickwickian sense* is the notion of inhabiting a universe with private semantics and exclusive membership. This joke is related to the infrastructure of *The Pickwick Papers*, and particularly to the design as first conceived by Dickens, who proposed at the outset to recount the adventures of a company of enthusiasts who are engaged on ludicrous projects, and who are 'Pickwickian' in their glorious innocence of the world and its ordinary meanings.

3·5 LOCATIVE FORMULAE

The components of what we are here calling 'formulae', or 'formulaic jokes' invite definition. Consider, then, the following, a fair specimen of the so-called 'Irish' joke:

> ***Did you hear about the Irish centre forward who missed a penalty but scored on the action replay*?**

This is a joke for the television age. Its locus is in the phrasal compound *action replay* – meaning 'repeat of the action recorded on TV film', but 'Irishly' interpreted as 'an actual repetition, a real second attempt'. The cream of the joke is the surreal implication that one *could* score a goal in this way if only one were 'Irish' enough. In Irishisms, as in the Pickwickian sense of things, there is the faith of innocence.

Recognition of a locus is partly a matter of consulting the mental dictionary that lists the relevant generic details, and in part a response to the general structure of the joke. A *location*, a phrasal siting of the locus, requires a matrix form. Some sort of preparation for the discharge of the joke, a *pre-location* (or *collocation*: see below) is necessary; and this pre-location may embody more than one significant or directive element:

PRE-LOCATION				LOCATION
Did you hear about	the Irish centre-forward	who missed a penalty	but	scored on the action replay?
Signal (of the intention to joke)	*Orientation* (to the type of joke)	*Context* (in which joke operates)		*Locus* (word or phrase which clinches or discharges joke)

What is illustrated here is a formula presenting in sequence all the elements of pre-location, *ie* the *signal* that a joke is intended, the *orientation* to a type of joke, and the *context*, or immediately relevant background to the joke.

The *signal* element is indispensable, and takes various forms. It may be a tag of the kind that is always recognized as introducing a funny story or a humorous observation (*eg* the propositional question 'Did you hear the one about. . .?', or the existential opening 'There's this fellow. . .); it may be the question that forewarns of a riddle ('What's a. . .?', 'How do you. . .?', 'How many. . .?' 'Where do. . .?'); it may be an echo of the cliché-imperative, 'Be *x*, Do *y*', beloved of publicists and copywriters (*eg*: *Be alert – England needs lerts*; *Help save our trees – eat a beaver*); it may be a quotation that has knocked about too long and has worn into a cliché (thus '*Hell hath no fury like a woman scorned*' yields *Hell hath no fury —— like a woman's corns* / —— *like a female jury* / —— *like a vested interest masquerading as a moral principle*). In short, there are forms of words that warn us of the advent of a joke, in some cases all the more emphatically because they are only used for joking purposes.

More widely, the signal of intent may embrace the whole form of the joke, as immediately perceived by the recipient. Many jokes are bedded in a fossil syntax, a received verbal structure that we recognize as belonging wholly or in the main to humorous practice. For example, the sentence-frame *Come back . . . all is forgiven* is used only with the intention to joke, and never in the straightforward, unironic expression of a wish. I may say, without mischievous purport, *I wish Oscar Wilde were alive and writing today*, but if I exclaim *Come back, Oscar Wilde, all is forgiven*, it will be understood that I speak with some sort of humorous implication.

Orientation is an element that may be omitted, or that may coincide with the declaration of a context. It indicates, as a rule, that the joke will belong to a thematic type, *eg* that it will be an 'Irish' joke, or a 'banana' joke, or a 'waiter' joke, or an 'elephant' joke ('*How d' you know if there's an elephant in the fridge?*' – '*Footprints in the butter*'). In a less specific way, the orientation of a joke may be established by peculiarities of language. For instance, the question *Why didn't the viper vipe 'er nose*? tells the addressee that this is going to be a joke about funny pronunciation, and that he is not to expect a quibbling answer such as *Because she thought she could wriggle out of it*, or a lunatic-logical response of the type *Because her hands were full*. (The answer is *Because the adder 'ad 'er 'andkerchief*.)

The *context* is the playing surface of the joke; a background, a condition, a set of limiting facts. In humour, as in usage generally, context may be verbally represented, or may be perceived extra-linguistically, in the understood situation or the general cultural assumption. It may be convenient to distinguish between the *defined* and the *implied* context. Jokes that are exhaustively formulated define a context, jokes that leave something to conjecture do not; indeed, some of the most effective jokes draw their strength from an element of the unstated. Often a joke that makes no extensive definition of context carries some word that briefly indicates contextual possibility; an example of such a *context marker* is discussed below.

Of the four elements represented in the diagram on *p* 34, two are obligatory in the construction of a formulaic, or *locative* joke: the signal of intent and – self-evidently – the locus. These occur in diverse sequences. A *headed sequence* follows the pattern *signal — locus*, the order one might posit if one were trying intuitively to describe the composition of a joke. However, 'signal' does not mean 'a joke follows'; it means 'interpret this' (*ie* what follows, what is contained, or even what precedes) 'as a joke'. Accordingly, in the formulation of some jokes the signal spans the locus (*spanning sequence*), while in another type (*tailed sequence*) the 'location' element actually begins the joke, like a statement of its theme, and the signal of intent follows, as a species of commentary. Not in all jokes, then, does the material complementary to the locus take the form of a *prelocation*; there are cases in which we could speak more appropriately of a *collocation*, or even an *allocation*.

These points may be elaborated with the help of two versions of the same joke. Version (a), *Come back, Guy Fawkes, all is forgiven* is an example of the spanning sequence:

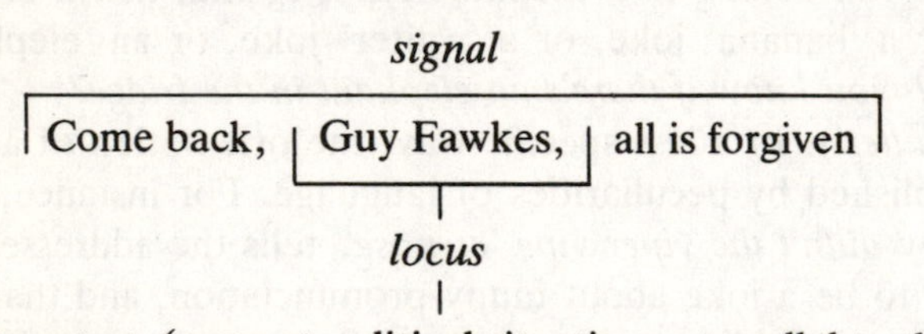

implied context: (present political situation as parallel to that of 1605)

There is no defined context; the context is what the originator and the addressee assume about the circumstances in which the joke is uttered. Nor is there any mark of orientation, unless we take it that this element here coincides with the signal of intent ('this is going to be one of those '*Come back*' jokes') The joke is formulated by means of a signal spanning a locus. It could in fact be reduced to the form of a headed sequence, *ie* the laconic *Come back, Guy Fawkes*, but ritually – and jokes are often ritual performances – we expect *all is forgiven* in completion of the signal.

Version (b) of the Guy Fawkes joke, *Guy Fawkes, where are you now that we need you*? has the tailed sequence pattern:

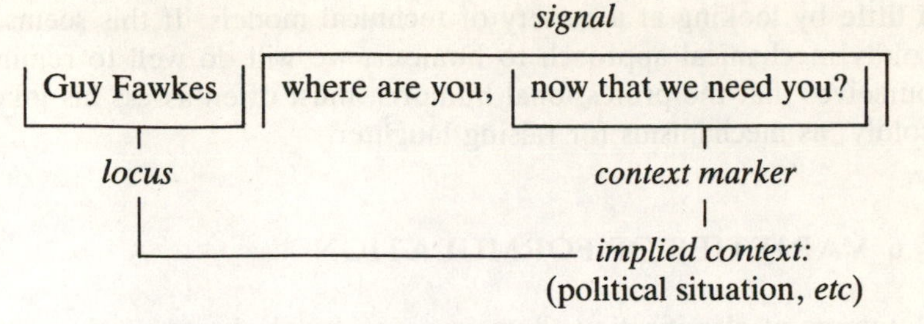

In formulation, this is a little more sophisticated than version (a), because it contains something that hints at a definition of context: the words *now that we need you* function automatically as a *context marker*, suggesting 'whatever state of affairs may be relevant to this particular use of the joke-formula'. The design of version (b) is thereby more elaborate, or possibly more 'pointed', than that of version (a), but it is not necessarily superior as a joke. The how and the when of the telling must also be taken into account.

Here arises a fascinating possibility: that of comparing the efficiency of rival formulations. There is obviously more than one way of telling a joke:

(a) *Did you hear about the Irish centre forward who missed a penalty and scored on the action replay*?

(b) '*Wasn't it a shame when Brendan missed the penalty*?' – '*Ah, God and the saints be praised, but he made no mistake with the action replay*.'

(c) '*Sure, what you lose on them penalties*,' *says Pat* '*you gain on them darling action replays*'

(d) *A smart centre forward called Finnegan,*
Desirous the Irish would win again,
  Missed the easiest shot
  From the penalty spot,
But the film replay put the ball in again.

Comparative strengths and weaknesses of formulation might point to a grading of these examples in order of effectiveness ('this raises a grudging laugh', 'this produces a knowing smile', 'I see that this is supposed to be funny'). Of course we cannot wholly judge the effectiveness of a joke without knowing something about the audience and the background of the telling, but we can perhaps learn a little by looking at a variety of technical models. If this seems a coldly mechanical approach to humour, we will do well to remind ourselves that the professional humorist must often assess his jokes coldly, as mechanisms for raising laughter.

3.6 VARIETIES OF FORMULATION

Attempts at classification, however, can hardly be more than tentative. The wheels are lively, and leap the categorical rails; compositional and semantic features overlap, and some simple types have complex variations. Our discussion of formulaic varieties is therefore rough-and-ready. It steers a course from one-liners to two-liners, and thence to rhymed forms, with digression and commentary as the need arises.

(a) Definitions and verdicts

These are one-liners with syntactic patterns typically involving the copulative verb (BE), though other verbs are possible. *A is B*, where *B* is, for example, a noun, a noun phrase, a noun plus prepositional phrase, a noun clause, a noun + conjunction or pronoun (*that*, *who*) + a clause. *A verbs B* where B is, for instance, a direct object or an adverbial adjunct. *A = B* where the equational process is expressed by a mark of punctuation, *eg* a colon, a dash, a comma.

Joking definitions and humorous verdicts share this syntactic network, and also have in common the frequent use of puns. Typical definitions:

(i) *The Eskimos are God's frozen people* (with a pun at the locus, on 'chosen people')

(ii) *Abstinence is the thin end of the pledge* (punning on 'thin end of the wedge')

(iii) *Karl Marx's grave – another communist plot* (punning on *plot* = 1 'conspiracy', and 2 'patch of ground')

Typical verdicts:

(i) *The DC 10 isn't all it's cracked up to be* (a 'black' pun on *crack up* = 'praise' and *crack up* = 'crash', with reference to the disastrous loss of a Douglas DC10 airliner at O'Hare airport, Chicago, in 1979)

(ii) *Education kills by degrees* (with a pun on *degrees*; note that what the verb expresses is a verdict rather than a definition)

There is an overlap between 'verdicts' and a type of accusation or complaint; see below, under group III (iii).

(b) Captions and annotations

These one-liners are like cartoon captions, or laconic remarks 'annotating' aspects of behaviour, current trends or events in politics, society and the arts, *etc*. There is an affinity, and sometimes an overlap, with witticisms of the 'verdict' type, though distinctions of syntax can be noted. Representative utterances, here somewhat impressionistically classified, are set out below in four groups; diverse as they may be, a family likeness is to be seen in the recurrence of personal pronouns, personal names, or in some cases indications of a profession or occupation. The 'caption' presents the world as viewed by an *I* looking at *you*, or at *him/her*, or at *people of that sort*.

Group I

('Quaint Conjectures')

(i) *Maybe the Joneses are trying to keep up with you.* (An inversion of the common phrase 'trying to keep up with the Joneses')

(ii) *I think sex is better than logic, but I can't prove it*

In these examples, a note of conjecture is sounded by *maybe* and *I think*, characteristic signals of this genus of joke. (Another variation is *Have you ever thought. . .?*) The pronoun *you* becomes the locus in example (i) as a result of inverting the popular phrase in which *the Joneses* stand for acquisitiveness, materialism, snobbery, status-seeking, *etc*. The inversion needs to be marked orally by a pattern of intonation and stress that puts a focusing accent on *you*. In example (ii) (a joke for frustrated or fallacy-fancying philosophers) the locus is obviously *prove*, with a reflection of the pre-locative *think*; here again, oral features of stress and intonation, counterpointing *think* and *prove*, bring out the point of the joke)

Group II

('Vexed questions')

(i) *Why is it that the only people capable of running this country are either driving taxis or cutting hair?*

(ii) *How will I know if I'm enlightened?*

In each case the signal is a query-phrase, *Why is it that. . .?*, *How will I know. . .?* In jokes of this kind the locus is semantically complex, a two (or more) stranded riddle. The point about taxi-drivers and barbers is that, to keep their clients and themselves amused, they talk a great deal, often about politics. In example (ii) *enlightened* is a locative pun, = (1) having knowledge, or the ability to obtain it, and (2) having acceptably 'liberal' attitudes.

Group III

('Complaints, accusations, grouses')

(i) *Stop the world, I want to get off.*

(ii) *Down with early Byzantine church music.*

(iii) *All this drinking will be the urination of me.*

Example (i) began life as a graffito, and became the title of a musical play; example (ii) is said to have been observed on a wall at the University of Edinburgh (it is a type of academic joke that either misfires completely or proves irresistibly funny). These examples have the characteristic interjection signals (*Stop /it/*, *Down with*) associated with common phrases or clichés (*Stop the bus*, *Down with capitalism*).

The point of (iii) (should it need explaining) is that *urination* is an inspired anagram of *ruination* – as in the periodic, paterfamiliar wail *All these phone bills / credit accounts / dental charges / price increases: etc / will be the ruination of me.*

Group IV

('Maxims, bywords, pseudoproverbs')

(i) *We have been standing on an economic precipice, and we have taken a great step forward.* (Said with reference to the policies of Mrs Thatcher's government)

(ii) *Give them the job, and they will finish the tools.* (Said with reference to technical aid for 'developing' countries, this sarcasm inverts the words of Winston Churchill's wartime appeal to the United States – 'Give us the tools and we will finish the job.')

(iii) *When the revolution comes, don't turn round.*

Such jokes are often political, and are generally marked (a) by expressions of time – *when*, *have been*, *will*, (b) by locative punning, eg: *turn round* = (1) 'look back', (2) 'revolve', *finish* = (1) 'complete', (2) 'destroy', and (c) by imperatives – *give them*, *don't*.

(c) Glossed Propositions

These are one-line jokes consisting of an enigmatic proposition followed by an explanatory comment. Often a form of insult, they depend heavily on the device of making semantic transfers from one field of usage to another. They are related to the two-line 'Text and Rejoinder' jokes discussed under (j) below.

(i) *Her face was like a million dollars – all green and crinkly.*
(ii) *You have a mind like a mineral railway – one-track and dirty.*
(iii) *A woman is like a piano. If she's not upright she's grand.*
(iv) *The days of graffiti are numbered – the writing's on the wall.*

Graphologically, the dash separating proposition and gloss is a mark of the type. The reader/listener recognizes the proposition as a signal of intent to joke, much as he recognizes the question-challenge of a riddle as the signal of intent. (All the above examples could be translated into riddling question-and-answer exchanges: 'Why is a woman like a piano?' 'Because. . .'*etc.*)

(d) Transforming tags

One of the easiest ways to signal a joke – indeed, to enforce the notion of joking when no joke is readily apparent – is to attribute a form of words to some dubious authority: *as the man said*. This device, which for centuries has been the resort of wags and wiseacres, now most commonly appears in the notorious *as the actress said to the bishop*, an interjection that makes leering innuendo out of the most innocent utterances. (*I do like Victorian design. . .*; *I wouldn't change it for anything larger . . .*; *Some of the fittings need attention . . .*; *The position is so convenient. . .*; *You have everything within reach. . .etc, etc, ad nauseam*)

A variant of *as the man said* enjoyed great popularity in the nineteenth century, taking general impetus, it seems, from the success of *Pickwick Papers*. The character of Sam Weller is typified by this kind of joke:

(i) *Wery glad to see you indeed, and hope our acquaintance may be a long 'un, as the gen'l'm'n said to the fi' pun' note.*
(ii) *Anything for a quiet life, as the man said wen he took the sitivation at the lighthouse.*

Though the form was not invented by Dickens, the name 'Wellerism' has been attached to it. Some American examples:

(iii) *I guess he'll re-wive, as the gentleman said when his friend fainted at his wife's funeral.*
(iv) *Short visits are best, as the fly said when he lit on the hot stove.*
(v) *'I'm at my wit's end,' said the king, as he trod on the jester's toe.*
(vi) *'A little will go a long way,' said the man, as he spit off the Woolworth building.*

Example (vi) proclaims the longevity of the type: a robust proverb from Tudor times runs *'Every little helps' quoth the wren when she piss'd in the sea.*

Wellerisms are delayed action jokes. They create their comic tension through a tailed sequence, the 'collocation' occurring at the end of the formula and containing in its ultimate item a crucial piece of contextual information:

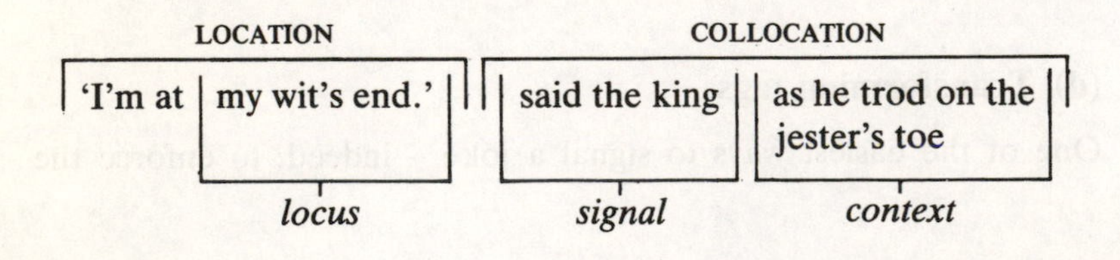

The joke is located in a form of caption – like the caption of a magazine cartoon – expressed as direct speech. The signal of intent always consists of a tag phrase, and the context-element usually provides the data for a retrospective wrench of meaning; so that here the recipient of the joke makes the corrective switch from *wit* = 'mental capacity' to *wit* = 'humorist', and from *end* = 'last resort' to *end* = 'extreme point or boundary of physical object'.

In some Wellerisms the context is defined in such detail that the point of the joke is virtually shifted – or rather, a new joke begins to grow, anecdotally, out of the matrix utterance. For example, the elder Weller is said by Sam to be

> *The wictim o' connubiality, as Bluebeard's domestic chaplain said, with a tear of pity, ven he buried him.*

Clearly, the joke lies primarily in the surprising equation of *the victim of connubiality* with *Bluebeard*; but the notion of Bluebeard having a domestic chaplain, and a tender-hearted one at that, raises anecdotal possibilities that threaten to make us forget the originating joke.

The recurrent tag is a device that can be used to effect the humorous transformation of an extended text. In *The Crowning Privilege*, Robert Graves tells how he once devastated a Tennysonian lyric by substituting the words *bottom upwards* for the refrain-invocation *Oriana*:

> They should have stabbed me where I lay,
> Oriana!
> How could I rise and come away,
> Oriana?
> How could I look upon the day?
> They should have stabbed me where I lay,
> Oriana –
> They should have trod me into clay,
> Oriana. [14; *p* 110]

This is a wicked illustration of the principle that a carefully selected tag can wreak havoc with the fine feelings of many a sober text.

(e) Catchword forms

There is a type of tag-joke in which the fixed element in the formula is a routine introductory wording, *eg*:

(i) *She was only a baker's daughter, but she never went short of dough*; updated alternative . . . *but she could always make the bread*. (The wording of jokes can change with the language itself, in this case with current slang; *dough*, once the knock-about word for 'money', has been overtaken and largely replaced by *bread*.)
(ii) *She was only a greengrocer's daughter, but she certainly knew her onions.*
(iii) *She was only a banker's daughter, but nobody made her a loan*. (With a ribald *double entendre* on *make* = 'have sexual relations with', and a pun on *a loan* = *alone*.)

The 'daughter' routine, obscure in origin, is conceivably an irreverent comment on nineteenth-century romantic iconography. Comely daughters abound in Victorian literature and balladry. Tennyson, for example, wrote poems on the topic of the gardener's daughter, the doctor's daughter, and the miller's daughter, and thought of writing one on the innkeeper's daughter. Echoed in *The Miller's Daughter* is the erotic theme of the young man attracted to a girl of lower social rank. (*And slowly was my mother brought / To yield consent to my desire / She wished me happy, but she thought / I might have looked a little higher*.) 'She was only a miller's daughter,' one might comment, 'though bred for a nobler role'; or perhaps, 'She was only a miller's daughter, but her soul was a fine white flower' – *etc*, *etc*.

Among other catchword forms are the 'Wanted' and 'They call' jokes, currently not much in evidence. 'Wanted' jokes make simple fun of everyday idiom:

(iv) *Wanted: coffins for the dead of night.*
(v) *Wanted: pockets for a coat of paint.*

The structure of these jokes is rudimentary: a conventional signal – *Wanted* – a context-defining term – *coffins* – and a locus – *the dead of night*. Reformed as a riddle, this might read: 'Where will you find the dead without a coffin?' – 'The dead of night', or 'What's still, lifeless, and unburied?' – 'The dead of night'. There is a close relationship between catchword forms and riddles, a relationship clearly signposted in the *because* of 'They call' jokes:

(vi) *They call her 'Checkers', because she jumps when you make a bad move*. (Alternative: *They call her 'End game', because she keeps you in check and you never mate.*)

(vii) *They call him 'Pilgrim', because every time he takes her out he makes a little progress.*

These are like one-line riddles, and also like glossed propositions (see (c) above. The propositional form 'Her face was like a million dollars – green and crinkly' can easily be translated into the catchword style, 'They call her 'Million Dollars' because. . .'*etc.*)

(f) Parodic Allusions

There are one-liners that allude wittily to some common saying or well-known piece of text. Punning and more or less cumbrous verbal substitutions are frequent:

(i) *Is this Mick Jagger that I see before me*? (Remarked by a friend observing one of Mr Jagger's now quite rare TV appearances. The literary reference is to *Macbeth*, I, vii, 33, 'Is this a dagger which I see before me?)

(ii) *Two's company, three's a deformity* (Graffito alluding scabrously to the sexual act; formula based on 'Two's company, three's a crowd'.)

(iii) *Red sky at night, shepherd's house is on fire.* (The British weather wisdom has 'Red sky at night, shepherd's delight'.)

Advertising slogans are frequently parodied, even by the advertisers themselves. The brewers of Heineken beer, for example, began their TV advertising campaign by proclaiming that *Heineken refreshes the parts most other beers don't reach*. The commercial playlets introducing this slogan have become more and more ingenious, until recently a fanciful copywriter produced a scenario depicting Wordsworth, in a Cumbrian landscape, moodily groping for the first line of *Daffodils* ('Er. . .er. . .*I was just strolling around, not doing very much*. . .er. . .er') and only finding it (*I wandered, lonely as a cloud*) after taking an inspiring draught of Heineken. This was followed by the clinching, pun-pretty line: *Heineken refreshes the poets most other beers don't reach*. Inevitably, the graffiti wits have taken up the theme; we find, for instance, that *Mavis Brown refreshes parts most beers won't touch*. In Britain, the advertising slogan is the new wit-object, to be tested, twisted, turned, much as the Elizabethans manipulated commonplace puns. An advertisement for

Smirnoff vodka, ringing the changes on the formula *I thought X was Y, until I discovered Smirnoff*, has spawned innumerable parodic variants, including one from the University of Exeter, bewailing the effects of 'scrumpy', the potent 'rough' cider of south-west England: *I thought nausea was a novel by Jean-Paul Sartre*, *until I discovered scrumpy*. ('Smirnoff' and 'Heineken' jokes now appear to have passed into the limbo of discarded copy.)

(g) Exhortations

Here is another type of joke that feeds parodically on the forms of public notices – in this case, on notices that nag us into exemplary behaviour. *Be Like Dad, Keep Mum*, ran the World War II poster warning Britons against careless talk. This theme of public-spiritedness is mocked in latterday imitations:

(i) *Be alert – England needs lerts*. (This has provoked the sequel-joke that comments, *No, we have too many lerts – be aloof*; which in its turn has begotten the retort *No, don't be aloof, there's safety in numbers – be alert*. A remarkable exercise in Humpty-Dumpty lexicography.)

(ii) *Help save our forests – eat more beavers*. (No comment.)

(iii) *Come home to a real fire – buy a cottage in Wales*. (A witty mix of adlanguage and political allusion. The slogan 'Come home to a real fire' figures on the advertisements of the National Coal Board; Welsh nationalists have burned down many 'second homes' and holiday cottages owned by English people.)

Exhortations are related in pattern to glossed propositions. As examples (ii) and (iii) may suggest, they frequently occur as a form of laconically pointed commentary on current social and political events.

(h) Jonathanisms

'Brother Jonathan' is the tall-ordering personifier of American folk humour. Jonathan says *X is so Y that Z*:

(i) *My uncle Sam is so tall that he has to climb a ladder to shave himself*.

(ii) *Our Lily's mouth is so big, she daren't laugh in case her head falls off.*
(iii) *He's so mean, he stands on one foot at a time, to save shoeleather.*

The structure consists of a declarative clause of the type Subject-BE-Complement (*my uncle is tall, her mouth is big, he's mean*), which is followed first by a result-clause (*/so that/ he has to climb a ladder, she daren't laugh, he stands on one foot at a time*) and then by an explanation-clause of infinitive or adverbial pattern (*to shave himself, in case her head falls off, to save shoeleather*). Jonathan's narrative logic notes a state of affairs, describes a result, and adds a reason. The first clause is the signal of intent and the orientation to a type of joke; the second clause amplifies contextual information supplied in the complement of the first clause; and the third clause is the location of the joke, the point at which strands of information (*he is tall, he uses a ladder*) are absurdly joined (*to shave*) This is one of those productive formulae, on which invention can freely elaborate (*eg*: *He's so forgetful, he ties a knot in his belt to remind himself why he tied the knot in his handkerchief*).

(i) False premises and flawed inferences

A form of academic humour is the logic-boggling one-liner that probes linguistic equivalences, ambiguities, and irregularities of semantic fit:

(i) *My doctor says if I do nothing for my cold it'll last for seven days, but if he treats it, it'll go away in a week.*

(ii) *Nothing is kinder to the hands than Fairy Liquid, so next time you wash the dishes, use nothing.* (Logicians themselves – Lewis Carroll is an eminent example – are given to the humour of attributing referential substance to *nothing*, or of treating *no* as a positive quantifier like *many*, *all*: *No trains arrive on time, so if you don't catch the express you should get there early.*)

(iii) *Forever goes quick*, OR *I'd like to spend eternity with you, if you can spare a moment.* (An oxymoron for lovers. From the humourless it always raises an exasperated query, 'How can *forever* be *quick*?', *etc*)

Of such examples it may be enough to say, at this point, that the locus of the joke coincides with the piece of text that defies the expected predication (*in a week*, *use nothing*, *quick*, *a moment*).

(j) Text and rejoinder

This two-line form is an expansion of the glossed proposition; it implies a dialogue between one who propounds and one who answers with mischievous comment:

(i) *The meek shall inherit the earth*
– *But not its mineral rights*

(ii) *The family that prays together stays together*
– *Thank God my mother-in-law's an atheist*

(The text is an evangelizing slogan, sometimes seen on church billboards)

(iii) *Lift under repair – use other lift* (Public notice)
– *This Otis regrets it's unable to lift today* (Scribbled addition)

(The comment is a brilliant parodic allusion to the refrain of the song 'Miss Otis regrets she's unable to lunch today.' Generic reference: Many of the lifts (elevators) in public buildings are manufactured by the Otis company)

(iv) *I love Margaret Holmes* (Graffito)
– *Good Lord, Watson, so do I* (Added in a different hand)

(An irresistible piece of buffoonery, with an 'invisible' prelocative joke, *ie* the assumed comma after *Margaret*, which would specify an intonation pattern and also predict an intonation in the rejoinder)

Public notices, religious texts, and mural avowals very often provide the ground for a joking retort. Because the 'text' is seriously intended, the signal of intent to joke comes late, breaking in with the joke itself. As often as not the signal is some phonetic feature (intonation, stress, loudness, a special timbre) reflected textually, *eg* in the form of an emphatic adversative (*but not*), an exclamatory phrase at the onset of the rejoinder (*Thank God*, *Good Lord*), or the words of a well-known melody (. . .*Otis regrets*. . .).

(k) Question and answer

The classic two-line form embraces riddles, comedian-and-straight-man jokes, and the whole schoolyard gallimaufry of bananas, elephants, waiters, what-do-you-dos and how-can-you-tells:

(i) *What do you get when you pour boiling water down a rabbit hole?*
– *Hot cross bunnies.*

(ii) *How can you tell the difference between a weasel and a stoat?*
– *Well, the weasel's weasily identified, and the stoat's stoatally different.*

(iii) *Why does the Prince of Wales wear red-white-and-blue braces?*
– *To keep his trousers up.*

(iv) *Waiter, is this a dead fly in my soup?*
– *Yes sir, it's the hot water that kills them.*

The question element is the immediately recognized signal of intent; it also includes a note of orientation, telling the listener/reader that this is going to be, for example, a 'How can you tell?' or a 'Waiter' joke. Challenged by the signal, the addressee obediently resigns himself to ignorance (only the stubbornly uncooperative try to find a reply). The answer then locates the joke. Example (i) clearly illustrates the structure:

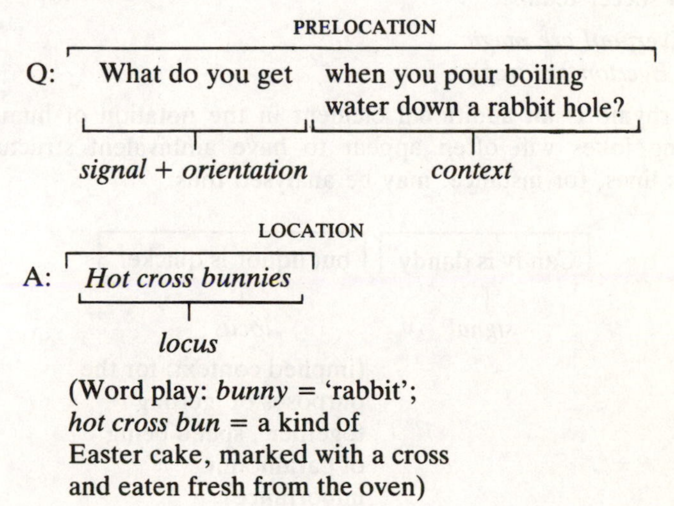

As a rule the answer element falls into one of two categories, *ie* the play on sound and meaning or the breach of logical/discursive expectations. Examples (i) and (ii) represent the word-play type; in (iii) and (iv) we have jokes about the predictability of discourse. The addressee in (iii) is entitled to suppose that *red-white-and-blue* is significant information, but the answer treats it as irrelevant. In (iv), the import of the question as a speech act is deliberately misread; it is clearly meant to be a complaint, but the waiter in the joke accepts it as a scientific enquiry. (Or possibly as a different species of complaint – NOT 'Why is this dead fly in my soup?' but 'Why is my fly dead?')

(l) Rhymed forms

Some formulaic jokes take prosodic shape in a rhymed couplet or quatrain. Rhyme may be a point of locative strength, as in Ogden Nash's slick verdict on the materials of courtship (the poem is entitled *Reflections on Ice-Breaking*):

Candy
is dandy
But liquor
is quicker

Or as in a text-and-comment antithesis, *eg* this graffito assessment of two soccer teams:

Liverpool are magic
– Everton are tragic

Since rhyme is an additional element in the notation of humour, rhyming jokes will often appear to have ambivalent structures. Nash's lines, for instance, may be analysed thus:

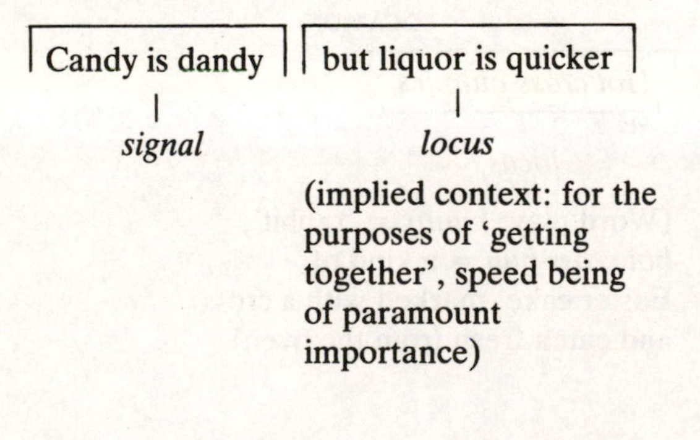

This suggests that the quatrain is the whole joke, with the first lines as a form of prelocation; *Candy is dandy* is text, *liquor is quicker*, rejoinder. It is possible, however, to set out the structure in a different way:

joke 1		+	*joke 2*	
PRELOC.	LOC.	but	PRELOC.	LOC.
Candy is	dandy		liquor is	quicker
signal (verdict-syntax)	*locus* (implied context: for elegant courtship)		*signal*	*locus* (implied context: for speedy seduction, speed being the important consideration)

Thus represented, the joke appears to be complex – a coordinated joke – and, so to speak, *plurilocative*; each line has its witty locus, and the two loci together constitute the point of the whole joke. There must be many such instances, in which rhyme not only decorates the humorous utterance, but also complicates it.

Rhyme lives in the ritual spell-castings and insults of the back alley (*Who's that coming down the street*? – *Mrs Simpson, sweaty feet*) with a crudity and a vigour that occasionally break out in literary epigram:

a politician is an ass upon
which everyone has sat except a man

Cummings' wisecrack fares uncertainly in Standard British English, where *ass* means only 'donkey', and a 'backside' is an *arse*. Note, however, the syntactic form of definition or verdict, and the characteristic punning, observable in other essays in the genre:

I am his Highness' dog at Kew;
Pray tell me, sir, whose dog are you?

(Pope's lines, inscribed on the collar of a dog belonging to the Prince of Wales. *Dog* = 1, 'canine animal', 2, 'lackey, functionary'.)

Satirical or merely silly quatrains abound, a recurrent theme being the joking epitaph with its vestigial narrative:

Poor Willie Brown lies here below,
His face you'll see no more;
Since what he took for H_2O
Was H_2SO_4.

Absurd though pedantic commentary may be, such rhymes will bear analysis, like any other formulation. The first two lines form the signal of intent and the orientation ('joke epitaph', 'little Willie joke'); the third line defines a context; and the fourth presents a locus (H_2SO_4) with the added emphasis of rhyme, and the graphological quirk of making a numeral represent a rhyming syllable (*4/more*).

Two short stanza types used exclusively for framing jokes are the clerihew and the limerick (possibly the only two wholly British contributions to the art of versification). The clerihew tells its off-beat tale with a defining context in the first two lines, and a locus in the rhyme of the second distich (though in fact we may discern a plurilocative pattern in the humour of the clerihew):

Alfred de Musset
Hated his pusset;
When it mieu'd
He mondieu'd.

This particular clerihew may be puzzling to persons of sober disposition who speak good French. The signal of intent is the whole form, recognized as soon as the recital reaches line 2; and the joke at all stages is reinforced by the increasingly outrageous rhyme and the ingeniously halting (shortening) rhythms.

The form of the limerick is also one that is recognized virtually from the moment the recital begins:

A gentleman dining at Crewe
Found quite a large mouse in his stew;
  Said the waiter, 'Don't shout
  And wave it about,
Or the rest will be wanting one, too!'

In the classic limerick, as practised by Edward Lear, it is a general rule for the last line to be a reflex of the first; *eg*, if the stanza begins 'There was an old fellow of X', it commonly ends 'That (adjective) old fellow of X'. In the modern development of the form, the usual pattern is the one represented in the example above, where the first two lines define a context (by naming a protagonist, line 1, and an attendant circumstance, lines 1/2); where the next two lines make an expansion of the context, often in the shape of 'what A or B then said'; and where the last line provides a location for the joke. Apparently the limerick is a kind of minimal anecdote, with all the marks of story-telling – the announcement of a theme, the account of things done and said, the statement of a conclusion. It would not be too difficult to produce an expanded prose version of our exemplary limerick, running to half a page or more, telling the same tale with small excursions, reflections, and additional stretches of conversation.

On the other hand, the joke in this limerick might easily be reduced in form. Recipes for brevity are available:

> *'Waiter, there's a mouse in my stew.'*
> *– 'Don't shout sir, they'll all be wanting one.'*
>
> *'A mouse in my stew! At Claridge's! How am I supposed to get rid of it?*
> *– 'Give it a good tip.'*
>
> *'Someone's bound to smell a rat', as the diner said when he found a mouse in his stew.*
>
> *The mouse in my stew was so big that when I pointed it out they charged me extra.*

Among formulaic jokes, the possibilities of equivalence and pattern-switching are considerable. This is how jokes survive and grow old and become veterans of many a company and campaign; this, too, is how the techniques of joking are explored, as formulae are replicated and expanded and revised and cross-connected with other formulae. However, something more than formulaic adroitness goes to the making of an anecdote or a comic narrative. The locative skill is important to the humorist, certainly; but beyond that is a narrative art that calls for marshalling powers of a different order.

Four

The design of the joke: (ii) the outgrowth of anecdote

4.1 THE REPLICATED JOKE

Some formulae are extremely successful, as productive mechanisms for word-play and witty definition; once established, they are seen or heard everywhere, and become, indeed, keywords to popular culture, expressing national instincts and obsessions. These verbal recipes often have non-humorous origins, *eg* in the patter of advertising or the slogan-making of politics. The slogan provides a syntactic or lexical pattern for the ingenious, perverse, and possibly outrageous operations of wit.

No formula illustrates this better than the so-called 'OK' joke. In its first manifestations the slogan-type *X rules, OK* was anything but comic. Scrawled or painted on walls and bridge-arches, it was an aggressive challenge in the street-warfare of rival factions; some believe it to have originated in the sectarian struggles of Northern Ireland, as an IRA slogan, *Provos rule, OK*. The 'OK' tag arrogantly reinforces its parent assertion, and hence is only occasionally followed by the question mark that would suggest 'do you understand?'; its common purport is 'this has to be accepted', or 'you'd better believe it if you know what's good for you'. (A sense of insult is unequivocally conveyed by a variant formula using the tag *yabas* = 'you bastards': *Hell's Angels rule, yabas.*)

Onto this unpromising stem much pleasant humour has been grafted. The social range of the formula was extended, first to include claims on behalf of neighbourhood football teams (*Rangers rule, OK?*) and then to make a game-object for college wits bent on political or academic word-play (as in *French diplomats rule, au Quai – ie* 'au Quai d'Orsay). Here is a short anthology of 'OK' graffiti, mainly of campus origin:

Cowardice rules – if that's OK with you
Procrastination will rule one day, OK?

Sceptics may or may not rule, OK
Pedants rule, OK – or, more accurately, exhibit certain of the trappings of traditional authority
Synonyms govern, all right
Roget's Thesaurus dominates, regulates, rules, OK, all right, agreed
Einstein rules relatively, OK
Heisenberg probably rules, OK
Schrödinger rules the waves, OK
Schizophrenia rules, OK, OK
Amnesia rules, O
Dyslexia lures KO
Apathy ru
Anarchy, no rules, OK
Royce Rolls, KO
Queensberry rules, KO
Hurlingham rules, croquet
French dockers rule au quai
Scots rule, och aye
Queen Elizabeth rules UK
Brunel rules IK
Town criers rule, okez, okez, okez
Kay Brown wears no knickers, ooh, Kay!
Personal problems rule, BO
Anagrams – or Luke?
Typographers rule, OQ

The formula is teased this way and that, in a competitive drive to exact from it all its humorous possibilities. Some of these examples can be understood quite easily by a foreigner knowing the general background of the formula and having an elementary competence in English. Others demand, for the uninitiated, a specific socio-cultural commentary (*eg* on the fact that the game of croquet is governed by a code called the Hurlingham Rules, or that English town criers – with a note on custom and costume – announce themselves in Old French, crying *oyez, oyez, oyez*); and some are clearly the inventions of academics at play (*eg* those alluding to Einstein and the Theory of Relativity, Heisenberg and the Theory of Probability, Schrödinger and Wave Theory). In several instances the 'stem' of the formula is playfully paraphrased or mutilated (*Synonyms govern,*

Dyslexia lures, Apathy ru, Anarchy, no rules, Royce Rolls: etc). In others it is the tag that suffers truncation, inversion, transformation (*eg*: *KO* = 'knockout', *UK* = 'United Kingdom', *IK* = Isambard Kingdom, the sonorous forenames of Brunel, the eminent Victorian engineer, *BO* = 'Body Odour', a phrase once coined by the adman for the benefit of the soap manufacturer). In others still, *eg: Anagrams – or Luke*?, ingenuity transforms both stem and tag. (The tag *or Luke* is an anagram of the words *rule OK*; this joke is effective only for devotees of English crossword puzzles, which have many anagrammatic clues.)

In all cases, however, the play of fancy is controlled by the limiting frame, the necessarily recognizable outline, of the formula. Within the framework, many joking permutations are possible, but no new *genus* is created; the 'family of the joke', so to speak, is not extended. There is no dependence of one joke upon another, and no protrusion of the self-contained joke-type into larger frames of reference. With some ingenuity we might conceivably force one or two of the examples listed above into a semblance of comic cross-talk:

Aggressive thin comic (flexing his muscles):	Queensberry rules?
Sly fat comic (backing away):	Cowardice rules . . .

Echoic retort is one way using a formula to extend the pattern of humour. But the limitations of this kind of invention are obvious; there is no larger possibility for the formula to become the seed and the flower of a profuse narrative outgrowth.

4.2 THE JOKE AS RECITAL

The *replicated* formula is self-limiting in its comic range. There is, however, such a thing as an *expanding* formula; the joke grows as it is re-told, with cumulative points that acquire force from a developing, progressively articulated context. This is well illustrated by an anonymous masterpiece called *The Academic Hierarchy*, which was in gleeful circulation, some years ago, among departmental secretaries at the University of Nottingham:

VICE CHANCELLOR
Leaps tall buildings in a single bound,
is more powerful than a locomotive,

is faster than a speeding bullet,
walks on water,
gives policy to God.

HEAD OF DEPARTMENT
Leaps short buildings in a single bound,
is more powerful than a shunting engine,
is just as fast as a speeding bullet,
walks on water if the sea is calm,
talks with God.

PROFESSOR
Leaps short buildings with a running start and favourable
winds,
is almost as powerful as a shunting engine,
is faster than a speeding bullet,
walks on water in an indoor swimming pool,
talks with God if special request is approved.

READER OR SENIOR LECTURER
Rarely clears a prefabricated hut,
loses a tug of war with locomotive,
can fire a speeding bullet,
swims well,
is occasionally addressed by God.

LECTURER
Makes high marks on the wall when trying to clear tall
buildings,
is run over by locomotive,
can sometimes handle a gun without injuring himself,
dog paddles,
talks to animals.

GRADUATE STUDENT
Runs into buildings,
recognizes locomotives two times out of three,
is not issued ammunition,
can stay afloat with a life jacket,
talks to walls.

UNDERGRADUATE
Falls over doorstep when trying to enter buildings,
says look at the choo-choo,

wets himself with a water pistol,
plays in mud puddles,
mumbles to himself.

DEPARTMENTAL SECRETARY
Lifts buildings and walks under them,
kicks locomotives off the tracks,
catches speeding bullets in teeth and eats them,
freezes water with a single glance;
She *is* God.

Hardly a narrative or an anecdote, this nevertheless has the cohesion of a sustained performance, in which one part depends on another. It is in effect a *recital*, based on a motif, like an air and variations in music. The root formula is a construction of the 'verdict' type (*A* = / *is* / *is defined by* / *B*; see § 3.5). Five such one-line verdicts make up a governing motif, expressing, at the outset, the following themes:

scope: 'leaps buildings'
strength: 'stronger than locomotive'
speed: 'faster than speeding bullet'
science: 'walks on water'
status: 'gives policy to God'

Subsequent repetitions – or rather imitations – of the motif then match, dependently and contrastively, each formulaic element; every variation is a joke on its predecessors – so that five jokes are running concurrently – and each completed 'motif' advances the progress of the master-joke, the tale of the hierarchy. In the process, the 'themes' noted above (*scope, strength, speed, science, status*) are gradually eliminated. The Lecturer has *scope* of a kind ('Makes high marks on the wall . . . *etc*'), plus a rudimentary *science* ('dog paddles') and a dubious *status* ('talks to animals'); but no *strength* to speak of '*is run over*') and nothing that can be defined as *speed* ('can sometimes handle a gun . . . *etc*'; only Professors and above have speed, though Readers and Senior Lecturers may initiate speed). The Graduate Student has neither *strength* nor *speed*, is virtually devoid of *science*, merely simulates a·*status*, has minimal *scope*. The Undergraduate is either totally inadequate or wretchedly irrelevant in every category. Through this thematic shaping, the recital becomes a kind of story, and it even has that property of the slick anecdote, the 'twist in the tail'. Narrative logic predicts an ending of the recital at the bottom of the academic ladder, but the final step reverses prediction; the lowest place in the hierarchy is thematically (in *scope-strength-speed-science-status*) the highest. Certain features of humorous narrative are missing here, but at least there is a strand of expectation, prediction, and continuity, to which we might assign the role of *plot*.

4.3 THE JOKE AS ROUTINE

'Recitals' such as *The Academic Hierarchy* are closely bound to an initiating pattern, or motif, repeated in each well-marked phase of the expanding performance. A looser but comparable form of organization is seen in the use of 'running jokes', with the help of which humorists and comedians build up their *routines*. In music-hall practice a 'routine' is the conventional structure of a sketch, monologue, *etc*; each routine has its typical gags, it costumes, its props. Translated into literary terms, the comic routine is the working and re-working of jokes that characterize the 'infrastructure' (see §3.3) of the narrative. A charming example is Stephen Leacock's *Sorrows of a Supersoul*, his parodic spoof on the dark romantic sensitivities of the 'Russian' novel. It is in the form of a diary kept by the heroine, one Marie Mushenough, the innocent subject of many jocund routines. Here is a typical extract:

Today

Otto touched me! He touched me!

How the recollection of it thrills me!

I stood beside him on the river bank, and as we talked the handle of my parasol touched the bottom button of his waistcoat.

It seemed to burn me like fire!

To-morrow I am to bring Otto to see my father.

But to-night I can think of nothing else but that Otto has touched me.

Next Day

Otto has touched father! He touched him for ten roubles. My father is furious. I cannot tell what it means.

I brought Otto to our home. He spoke with my father, Ivan Ivanovitch. They sat together in the evening. And now my

father is angry. He says that Otto wanted to touch him.
Why should he be angry?
But Otto is forbidden the house, and I can see him only in the meadow.

Two Days Later

To-day Otto asked me for a keepsake.
I offered him one of my hatpins. But he said no. He has taken instead the diamond buckle from my belt.
I read his meaning.
He means that I am to him as a diamond is to lesser natures.

This Morning

Yesterday Otto asked me for another keepsake. I took a gold rouble from my bag and said that he should break it in half and that each should keep one of the halves.
But Otto said no. I divined his thought. It would violate our love to break the coin.
He is to keep it for both of us, and it is to remain unbroken like our love.
Is it not a sweet thought?
Otto is so thoughtful. He thinks of everything.
To-day he asked me if I had another gold rouble.

Next Day

To-day I brought Otto another gold rouble.
His eyes shone with love when he saw it.
He has given me for it a bronze kopek. Our love is to be as pure as gold and as strong as bronze.
Is it not beautiful? [20]

The sections, or 'diary entries' are spanned by linking jokes. One of these is a piece of Leacockian fun with the presentation of the text in the diary form. Marie sometimes 'dates' her observations subjectively, as diarist – *eg*: *This Morning* – but more often uses the objective dating of an external observer – *eg*: *Next Day, Two Days Later*. A point of incidental interest about this narrative is that it exploits 'generically' the interplay of form and humorous content (see §2.6); the sense of timing in the management of the jokes depends largely on the diary technique of jotting short sentences on separate lines.

Apart from the 'date' joke, two sequences, or routines, span the passage. Of these, the first exploits the hoary old play on *touch* = (a) 'make physical contact with', and (b) 'borrow money from'. This punning could be reduced to a one-line gag, in the style of the variety comedian:

> *She said she wouldn't let me touch her for all the money in the world, so I touched her Daddy for ten dollars.*

And indeed, this is the formulaic root of Leacock's fun. He, however, expands the formula in his own characteristic fashion, making his heroine rejoice ludicrously in one kind of touching (*the handle of my parasol touched the bottom button of his waistcoat*) while she remains woefully ignorant of the other kind (*I cannot tell what it means*). The joke of 'meaning' – that is, of Marie's elaborate inability to perceive the obvious – runs through the entire piece; in our extract it is represented by her comments *I cannot tell what it means, I read his meaning, I divined his thought.*

The second sequence of jokes runs through the last three 'entries' in our extract. Here the root notion might be expressed as a text-and-rejoinder or question-and-answer formula (see §3.6 (j) and (k)):

A: *Take money from a woman*? *Shame on you*! *Is that any way to show your love*?
B: *Well, it shows how DEAR I am, doesn't it*?

(This chestnut was a-growing in Shakespeare's time. Fabian says to Sir Toby, 'This is a dear manakin to you, Sir Toby' – referring to Sir Andrew Aguecheek. Sir Toby replies, 'I have been dear to him, lad, some two thousand strong or so.') In Marie's diary the ancient joke about the values of love versus the values of the bank balance (as in *Diamonds Are A Girl's Best Friend*) is bedded in the other running joke, about meaning and perception. Marie 'reads' Otto's meaning, and obligingly practises a confidence trick upon herself. Her perception of Otto's supposed symbolism is so naively assured that eventually she does not even bother to announce explicitly *I read his meaning*. On being given the bronze kopek, she expresses her self-deception with oblique modality – 'Our love *is to be* as pure as gold and as strong as bronze.'

Marie is the wide-eyed victim of the repeated and interlinked jokes, but she is something slightly more than a simple knockabout. Through the humour of her victimization, and of Otto's venality, we begin to perceive the emergence of comic character and situation. Mere caricatures though she and Otto may be, they are nonetheless an advance on the lay figures of the stage comedian's stock – *eg* the nagging mother-in-law, the idle husband, the spendthrift wife. They are contributors to a developing plot, based on a run of jokes. Also associated with the pattern of humour are observations on what is said or thought, and expressions of judgement and interpretation – not least those making appeal to the reader. (*Is it not beautiful*?) The parody thus embraces primary features of narrative – actors, train of events, direct or indirect speech, interpretative pronouncements – but it is still not quite the kind of narration that we would characterize as *anecdote*. It is a mimetic routine, like a stage 'turn', in which the narrator embodies the narrative; in anecdote, the narrator presents the tale quasi-objectively (even though he may be involved in it) and has recourse to somewhat different modes of construction.

4.4 THE PATTERNED ANECDOTE

Here is a fairly well-known 'golf' story:

> The vicar, who enjoyed his golf, went down to the club one Monday afternoon, and found the place almost deserted. The only person there to give him a game was Billy Benson.
>
> Billy's trouble was that he was very bad at golf, and very profane. Nothing would go right for him. His approach shots were pathetically bad, and he couldn't succeed in sinking a simple putt. And every time the ball rolled past the hole, he said, 'Hell and damnation. Missed.'
>
> The vicar put up with this for some time, but at last he said, 'Look, Benson, would you mind not swearing.' Billy promised to curb his tongue, but at the very next hole he fluffed the easiest of putts, from two feet. 'Hell and damnation. Missed.' he said.
>
> Now the vicar was really annoyed. 'Look here, Benson,' he said, 'if you swear like that again, God will hear you, and a thunderbolt will come from on high and strike you down.' Billy resolved to clean up his language and improve his golf. At the next hole, therefore, he took particular trouble with his putt. He walked all round the ball, he raked away fallen

leaves, he laid his putter on the grass and got down and squinted along it. At last, after a few practice shots, he addressed the ball and struck it very gently. It rolled straight and true, and stopped one inch from the hole. 'Hell and damnation! Missed!' cried Billy Benson. And out of the sky shot a ball of lightning. And hit the vicar.

Then from on high came a mighty voice saying, 'Hell and damnation. Missed.'

The pattern of this anecdote is clear from the outset to anyone who has ever heard, or told, a fairy tale; it is the old ritual of three occurrences plus the crucial consequence. Thus:

Phase 1:	Billy Benson swears	– the vicar protests
Phase 2:	Billy Benson swears again	– the vicar warns of God's lightning
Phase 3:	Billy Benson swears for the third time	– God's lightning strikes – but hits the vicar

Many humorous anecdotes adopt this kind of phasing, generally suggestive of the 'external' viewpoint of a narrator who is not involved in the plot and is free to demonstrate to his audience the compulsive symmetry of events. (On symmetry and prediction, see §3.2.) The user of this conventional frame can fill out the scheme at will, supplying information or interpretative comment, providing significant adverbial pegs – so to speak – of time or place, and telling his audience what the characters say. It is, indeed, the speech-element, in the shape of the fatal comment, *Hell and damnation. Missed*, that conspicuously frames the narrative, marking off the phases till they culminate in a joke that might be expressed as a one-liner with a transforming tag (see § 3.6(d)): *He'll be sorely missed, as God said when the thunderbolt hit the vicar*. (Many anecdotes can be compressed formulaically, and many formulaic jokes can be expanded anecdotally.)

If we take it that the essential elements – the scaffolding members, as it were – of this anecdote are (a) the pieces of information that mark the onset of successive phases, (b) the adverbial 'pegs' that locate the story from phase to phase, and (c) the speeches of the characters, we might represent its framing as follows:

Introduction
Opening informs: *The vicar, who enjoyed his golf . . . etc.*
Adverbial pegs: *down to the club, there.*

Phase 1

Opening informs:	*Billy's trouble was that he was very bad at golf . . . etc*
Adverbial pegs:	*every time, past the hole*
Ends:	*'Hell and damnation. Missed.'*

Phase 2

Opening informs:	*The vicar put up with this for some time, but . . .* + speech to Billy
Adverbial pegs:	*at the very next hole*
Ends:	*'Hell and damnation. Missed.'*

Phase 3 + Conclusion

Opening informs:	*Now the vicar was really annoyed* + speech to Billy.
Adverbial pegs:	*at the next hole, one inch from the hole, out of the sky*
Pausing informs:	*And hit the vicar*
Ends:	*'Hell and damnation. Missed.'*

Reference to the text of the anecdote will show that the filling out of the frame is longer and more elaborate from Phase 1 to Phase 2, and from Phase 2 to the end of Phase 3; there is a deliberate retarding of the narrative before its climax – a common enough feature, perhaps, of the story-teller's art. Even a trifle such as this, evidently, is a small piece of fiction, with fiction's customary elements and fiction's conscious craft. The simple joke develops into the humorous fantasy. We may, of course, criticize the efficiency of the narration, but if we do, our attention is no longer concentrated on the merits of rival *formulae* (see, for example, §3.5), but on the viability of anecdotal *structures* and the appropriateness of the *style*.

4.5 'FREE' ANECDOTAL STRUCTURE

Fairy-tales, folk-stories, parables and popular yarns frequently have structures that enable an audience to predict the course of a narration, follow its turns, and anticipate the sort of outcome it will have. Thus there is a high degree of predictability in the framing of our 'golf' anecdote, and possibly this is an important part of the pleasure it is intended to afford; the listener becomes involved in the process of joke-making. In literary narrative of a more ambitious kind, anecdotes are as a rule more flexibly constructed, and their turns and transitions are not so clearly evident. Though guidelines certainly exist, the literary art consists in masking them, presenting what is on the face of it a casually-told tale.

Some books are constructed anecdotally, in a loosely-linked series of short narratives that arise out of, and in many cases make 'infrastructural' comment on, the central theme. Such a book is *Three Men In A Boat*. The principal episodes are festooned with anecdote; so adeptly, in fact, does Jerome manage his method of deliberate digression, that the anecdotes sometimes grow out of one another, or even cluster *within* one another, a short anecdotal comment interrupting a larger anecdotal process. Here, from the first chapter of the book, is an example of Jerome's narrative method. The 'three men' of the title discuss ways of spending a holiday, and one of them, Harris, suggests a sea trip. Jerome then sets in train a series of anecdotes, of which this is the second:

> Another fellow I knew went for a week's voyage round the coast, and, before they started, the steward came to him to ask whether he would pay for each meal as he had it, or arrange beforehand for the whole series.
>
> The steward recommended the latter course, as it would come so much cheaper. He said they would do him for the whole week at two-pounds-five. He said for breakfast there would be fish, followed by a grill. Lunch was at one, and consisted of four courses. Dinner at six – soup, fish, entree, joint, poultry, salad, sweets, cheese, and dessert. And a light meat supper at ten.
>
> My friend thought he would close on the two-pounds-five job (he is a hearty eater), and did so.
>
> Lunch came just as they were off Sheerness. He didn't feel so hungry as he thought he should, and so contented himself with a bit of boiled beef, and some strawberries and cream. He pondered a good deal during the afternoon, and at one time it seemed to him that he had been eating nothing but boiled beef for weeks, and at other times it seemed that he must have been living on strawberries and cream for years.
>
> Neither the beef nor the strawberries and cream seemed happy, either – seemed discontented like.
>
> At six, they came and told him dinner was ready. The announcement aroused no enthusiasm within him, but he felt that there was some of that two-pounds-five to be worked off,

and he held on to ropes and things and went down. A pleasant odour of onions and hot ham, mingled with fried fish and greens, greeted him at the bottom of the ladder; and then the steward came up with an oily smile, and said:

'What can I get you, sir?'

'Get me out of this,' was the feeble reply.

And they ran him up quick, and propped him up, over to leeward, and left him.

For the next four days he lived a simple and blameless life on thin Captain's biscuits (I mean that the biscuits were thin, not the captain) and soda-water; but, towards Saturday, he got uppish, and went in for weak tea and dry toast, and on Monday he was gorging himself on chicken broth. He left the ship on Tuesday, and as it steamed away from the landing-stage he gazed after it regretfully.

'There she goes,' he said, 'there she goes, with two pounds' worth of food on board that belongs to me, and that I haven't had.'

He said that if they had given him another day he thought he could have put it straight. [17; *pp* 12–14]

The style is casual, the narrative seemingly put together without too much thought for niceties of construction. A little study will show, however, that it is very carefully designed, and that its patterning takes us a stage or two forward from the rudimentary and plainly-marked structure of the golfing anecdote in §4.4.

In one respect, the shaping of the text is made quite obvious to the reader. There are four sentences that are given the typographical status of paragraphs:

(a) *My friend thought he would close on the two-pounds-five job (he is a hearty eater) and did so*

(Note the commercial metaphor in *close on*, and the tradesman/salesman sense of *job*. Compare this with 'verdict' formulae such as 'It's the sort of restaurant where you negotiate for a holding in the menu', or 'You have to take out a mortgage to eat there.')

(b) *Neither the beef nor the strawberries and cream seemed happy either – seemed discontented like*

(This is an echoic retort to the *contented* of the preceding paragraph: *contented himself with a bit of boiled beef and some strawberries and cream*. It suggests a question-and-answer formula: 'Were you unhappy on your trip?' – 'No, but my lunch was.')

(c) *And they ran him up quick, and propped him up, over to leeward, and left him.*

(The heartless verbs echo the passenger's own cry:

	'*Get*	*me*	*out*',	he said
so they	*ran*	*him*	*up*	
and	*propped*	*him*	*up*	
and	*left*	*him*		

A prudent traveller will of course always spew to *leeward*)

(d) *He said that if they had given him another day he thought he could have put it straight*.

(*Put it straight* suggests settling an account. We return to commercial metaphor, or to the humorous notion of eating as a form of business transaction. Although the word *settle* is never mentioned, the notional interplay of *settle the bill* and *settle the stomach* expresses the joke that motivates the narrative.)

The four typographically foregrounded sentences have more than one function in the framing of the narrative. In the first place, they mark the boundaries of episodes or phases within the anecdote. Thus Phase I describes the gargantuan menu (gargantuan, surely, even by Victorian standards), Phase II describes the first onset of unease, after a remarkable lunch with a *bit* of boiled beef and *some* strawberries (nowhere is it directly suggested that the greedy passenger has only himself to blame for being so set on getting his money's worth), and Phase III describes how the traveller succumbs to seasickness. Each of these phases concludes with a typographically distinct comment or summary, as in sentences (a), (b), and (c) above. Phase IV, the second part of the story, has the adverbially-pegged structure of plural occurrence (*for the next four days, towards Saturday, on Monday, on Tuesday*), making a link with the phrase *for a week's voyage* in the opening sentence of the story. This phase also concludes with a summarizing one-sentence paragraph, *ie* sentence (d) above.

These sentences are important, then, as framing members, lodged in the narrative in a fashion not unlike that of the repeated motif (*Hell and damnation. Missed*) of the golfing anecdote. They have, however, the further role that each is in some way a commentary on the immediately foregoing text. In one case there is a clear verbal link (*contented – discontented*), in others the connection is less direct but is nonetheless evident; for example, sentence (d), the sentence with which the narrative concludes, is a continuation in indirect speech, or 'author speech', of a summarizing comment made in direct speech, or 'character speech' ('*There she goes,' he said . . . etc*; *He said that if . . . etc*). This final sentence, furthermore, expresses the general humorous concept, or *root joke* of the anecdote; so that each commentary-sentence takes its own portion of text into scope, while the final commentary embraces the whole.

A further characteristic of the framing sentences is that each is humorously turned, making a joke or the likeness of a joke:

> *My friend thought he would close on the two-pounds-five job (he is a hearty eater), and did so.*

There is an impish appeal about the parenthesis, if we consider what it refers to: the multiple and bizarrely mingled courses of breakfast, lunch, marathon dinner, and that light meat supper. Also, though the sentence may elude classification as a locative formula, it contains something like a prelocation and a locus in the phrase '*close on* the two-pounds-five *job*'; there are items of vocabulary that locate the humour in a generic substructure. The other sentences present comparable features of construction and vocabulary; they may not be jokes in a formal sense, but they are nonetheless jokey. These sentences that mark out a structure, comment on the text, and have their own quality of jokiness, are a new feature in our account of humorous narrative. If a name is needed, let us call them *formulates* – because they are clues to the formulation of the narrative, because they formulate judgements, reflections, comments, *etc*, on the story, and because they are often worded in a pungently emphatic way that reminds us of the locative formula.

The construction of Jerome's narrative, set out schematically on *pp* 66–7, is almost as regular as the pattern of a folk-tale. What creates the impression of a casually-told story, distracting attention from the structural regularity, is the vivacious mischief of the style, with its ostensibly casual effects that are in fact so carefully planted and cultivated. Scrupulous attention is paid to sentence length – there is a particularly good example in the last sentence of the second paragraph (*And a light supper at ten*), with its wryly laconic form and 'afterthought' rhythm. Sardonic understatement, or sardonic displacement of meaning, mark some choices of word ('He *pondered* a great deal during the afternoon' = 'He felt queasy'; 'the announcement *aroused no enthusiasm* within him' = 'it made him feel sick'). There are carefully contrived echoes: the hero *contents himself* with beef and strawberries, but later the beef and strawberries *seem discontented*. There are also adroit contrasts or matchings. The odour of onions, *etc*, is said to be *pleasant*, but the smile of the wordly-wise steward is *oily* – and is purportedly the ultimate cause of the hero's malaise. As it proceeds, Jerome's narrative grows semantically complex, especially in its cultivation of irony. We know that *pleasant* is ironically intended, but how do we know? Is it because incompatible references are collocated, *ie* because *odours* are never *pleasant*? Is it because we make the empirical inference that the mingled smell of onions, hot ham, fried fish and greens must be anything but *pleasant*? Is it because *pleasant* should refer to the steward, and *oily* to the cooking smells, but that there is, so to speak, a reversal of roles?; the *odours* are personified – host-like, they *greet* the unfortunate traveller, before the steward, spoiling this good impression, *comes up* with his oily smile. Or is it because we respond immediately to all of these things – to our knowledge of familiar collocations, to the remembered experience of cooking smells, to our perception of a joke lying skin-deep in the text? ('Did the stew and greens make you sick?' – 'No, it was the steward's grins').

In the fourth phase of the anecdote there are several instances of Jerome's technique of flourishing the ostensibly loose word with precise comic effect:

(a) 'towards Saturday, he *got uppish*'
(b) '. . . *went in for* weak tea and dry toast'
(c) 'on Monday he was *gorging himself* on chicken broth'

All of these are comic mis-collocations. The arrogant, the insolent, the pretentious, the bully, the parvenu, are *uppish*; hardly the invalid. One *goes in for* strenuous physical pursuits, examinable courses of study, elaborate hobbies, costly possessions; hardly for weak tea and dry toast. *Gorging* is appropriate to chocolate, to pâté, to pork pie, to roast beef, to any rich or substantial food, but not really to chicken broth. There is a comic force in the totally inappropriate word – but the felicity of the choice does not end there. In each case, the extravagantly wrong expression rightly defines something in the character and behaviour of a convalescent: the reviving cheerfulness, the keen relish of the simplest experiences, the glad indulgence of elementary appetites. Thus *uppish* is funny, (a) because it is *not* the word for an invalid, and (b) because, after all, it *is* the word for an invalid, when he begins to sit up and take notice of the world about him.

It is this meticulous cultivation of style that most obviously distinguishes the literary anecdote from the narrative of popular culture – the jokes told in pubs and clubs, the strip-cartoon sequence, the folk tale in the oral tradition. Humorous narrative in the popular vein necessarily marks its presentation with readily perceptible conventions of structure and expression. Literary anecdote, with its apparently 'free' structure, both acknowledges and revises conventional methods of patterning, and allows for the play of individual creativity in style.

4.6 TOWARDS THE LARGER FORM

We are as yet a long way from the point at which we might begin to account for the larger linguistic patterns of comedy, and indeed we may question whether that point could ever be reached in a brief study. Some reflections present themselves, however, in connection with the terms *locative formula* (or *formulaic joke*), *formulate*, and *root joke*. These are important (and interrelated) features of extended comic narrative, and it may be said speculatively that the particular character of any piece of comic writing derives from the way in which these features are exploited or brought to the reader's attention.

In humorous short stories and comic novels, locative formulae are not as a rule the direct utterances of the author, or 'external' narrator. The formulaic joke is generally assigned to a character in the story, and therefore emerges in character-speech. There is an example in Jerome's anecdote. The queasy traveller finds time in his misery to turn the locative formula:

'What can I get you, sir?'
– 'Get me out of this',

to which the external narrator adds his comment, or *formulate*:

> And they ran him up quick, and propped him up, over to leeward, and left him.

From this is would appear that the locative formula in literary narrative can have artistic functions that transcend the making of an occasional joke. Like other elements of dialogue, it may illustrate a character or a situation, or be in some way connected with the infrastructure of the story (see below, on the matter of the *root joke*). These observations apply equally well to the case of first-person narratives; the 'I' of the story is a character like any other, whose wisecracks and witticisms take their place in the pattern of information about personalities and situations. A narrating 'I' may be full of smart, self-revealing turns of humour; or may be a rather humourless person who is sometimes unconsciously witty; or may lay out a whole comic narrative without one example of a formulaic joke.

If in fiction the locative formula becomes an attribute of funny characters (who are sometimes characterized by their formulae – *vide* the Wellers, father and son), authorial humour may be compensatingly expressed through the commentary devices we have called *formulates*. These utterances often call to mind, or can be paraphrased by, formulaic jokes. Some examples have suggested themselves incidentally, in the discussion of the Jerome anecdote. It seems that we have psychological access to stocks and patterns of joking, and that in our experience of humour we make connective reference to this stock. This often makes for a peculiar resonance in the reading of humorous narrative, when the reader creates a relationship between an actual piece of text and a recollected joke or a verbal parallel that seems appropriate to the narrative but that does not appear in so many words in the story. The resonance is all the more powerful when the author's formulates pick up the sense of the characters' locative formulae.

In Jerome's anecdote the formulates occur regularly, as framing devices. Their structural role is apparent because of the comparative brevity of the anecdote. The larger the scale of the comedy, the less easy it becomes to establish a patterned use of the formulate, or to do more than guess at its relevance to certain types of comic narration (*eg* those with strong moralizing overtones). Jane Austen's *Pride and Prejudice* opens with a famous sentence that has all the earmarks of a formulate:

> It is a truth universally acknowledged, that a single man in possession of a good fortune must be in want of a wife.

Here is a comic aphorism, witty in itself, inviting the reader to locate mischievous emphases on *universally* and *must*. Beyond that, however, this trenchantly formulated remark is an emblem of the whole comedy of marriage and manners and misconceptions, the entire *infrastructure* of *Pride and Prejudice*. When such an infrastructure has comic potential, or can be expressed humorously, we may refer to the workings of this informing spirit as the *root joke*.

An instance of a modern novel in which the reader is constantly made aware of the root joke, is Joseph Heller's *Good as Gold*. This is the story of Bruce Gold, an American Jewish academic with a hearty appetite for gentile women and a strong aspiration to gentile social status and political power. In the first chapter, Gold is commissioned by a friend to write a book on 'The Jewish Experience In America'. The subject fascinates him, but the challenge baffles him. 'I wouldn't know where to begin', he reflects. The search for a beginning is put off, however, while Gold embarks on a near-career as a prospective White House adviser. Not surprisingly, he has some difficulty in maintaining his identity in two worlds with different customs, different presuppositions, different systems (it seems) of logic: the Jewish world of his family and long-standing friendships, and the socially exclusive, self-assured, dismissively gentile world of the cultural and political establishment. The two worlds operate different codes; Gold virtually loses the key to one, and never succeeds in cracking the other, though he willingly submits himself to any absurdity, any humiliation, to have the chance of doing so. Throughout his ordeal, his perceptions are at once acute and opaque; for example, he continually rages against his *bête noire*, Henry Kissinger – even going to the length of making up a dossier of condemnatory newspaper clippings – apparently without realizing that the flaws he detects in Dr Kissinger are pre-eminently the flaws of Dr Gold. After more than 400 pages of narrative, Gold, his diplomatic aspirations abandoned, is still wondering how to begin the promised book on the Jewish Experience; the last words of the story are *Where could he begin*? The joke – the root joke of the book, adumbrated in one episode after another – is that the whole sorry/comic saga of Gold's attempts to come to adaptive grips with gentility is in itself an epitome of the Jewish Experience in America, a fact that Gold either cannot or will not see. On the final page is a brief episode that perfectly embodies the point. Gold watches a group of Jewish seminarists – students at a *yeshiva*, a religious school – playing baseball. They play the American summer game, but it happens to be winter. They wear *yarmulkas*, not baseball caps. Instead of the clipped hair of the baseball player, they have sidelocks – but some of the sidelocks are blond or ruddy, framing faces that look more Irish than Jewish. The game is suspended while an argument rages, and in the heat of the argument these religious seminarists mingle Yiddish words with American obscenities. Gold smiles at the contrariness of the scene, the Jewish stubborness of playing baseball in winter, but it does not occur to him that this is the very image of what he wants to write about. He turns away, still brooding over the promised book, still asking himself *Where could he begin*?

Joseph Heller's narrative power ensures that even a foreign reader can hardly miss the root joke of *Good as Gold*. Much of the stringent, mocking humour of the story, moreover, is articulated in the verbal games and lunatic logics for which this author seems to have a particular fondness (some examples are given in Ch. 6 below); so that a firsthand sociological knowledge of American culture, whether in its gentile or its Jewish manifestations, is not a prerequisite to the general understanding of the book. The fact remains, however, that *Good as Gold*, like other comedies, does reflect a society, a history, an experience, and is consequently full of allusions and hints of parody which give depth to the joke, but which are in great measure lost to the outsider. Problems of narrative structure may be mastered, but the teasing allusiveness of humour and the parodic challenge of comedy are difficulties (or delights, according to one's point of view) that persist.

Five

Allusion and parody

5.1 THE CONTROLLING ALLUSION

Allusion in the very broadest sense is never absent from our discourse; always there is some fact of shared experience, some circumstance implicit in the common culture, to which participants in a conversation may confidently allude. For families, friends, neighbours, colleagues, there is a generic knowledge of the affairs of the day – of politics, of social questions, of sports and entertainments, of current notions and phraseology. Such knowledge informs a good deal of what we say to each other, making its point even when its presence is veiled.

What we commonly understand by 'allusion', however, is something more explicit and overt, something for which the word 'citation' might be a more accurate name. These citations often have a function that goes beyond the mere decoration of a conversational exchange. They are a kind of test, proving the credentials of the initiated, baffling the outsider. In effect, they are a device of power, enabling the speaker to control a situation and authoritatively turn it to his own advantage.

The story is told of Jonathan Swift, that he was once present at a reception where he witnessed a peculiar mishap. On a table lay a violin, which was caught up in the skirts of a lady's gown and fell to the floor. Swift's reported response was a brilliant bilingual pun, in the form of a citation from Virgil's ninth Eclogue: *Mantua, vae, miserae nimium vicina Cremonae*, 'Alas, Mantua, too close a neighbour to wretched Cremona'. Only by patient cultural reconstruction can the twentieth-century reader work out the allusive purport of this line, which ostensibly refers to the resettlement of army veterans in the Roman provinces, with the consequent eviction of the unfortunate natives. (Cremona was the principal victim, but Mantua, Virgil's birthplace, lay nearby and shared the taint of having supported the wrong party in a civil war.) What, we may ask, has this plangent cry to do with violins? The point is, that Swift cleverly made the Virgilian line designate objects of his own time and culture. 'Mantua' was the name for a kind of loose gown, and Cremona – the home of Antonio Stradivari – was renowned for the skill of its violin makers. Thus, 'Mantua, too close, alas, to wretched Cremona', was Swift's punning comment on the tale of a flounce and a fiddle.

A brilliant joke indeed, for those who could understand it – and it is worth reflecting on the kind of audience on whom this virtuosity was practised. For many of those present, in that classically educated age, Virgil's words would certainly have the familiarity of a schoolroom text. It must be remembered, though, that schoolrooms and tutors were in the main for the sons of the well-to-do, who learned their Latin as a staple of rhetoric, an element in the curriculum of power. From this scheme of education, women and servants were generally excluded. (Eighteenth-century records do make some mention of learned ladies; Dr Johnson remarks that his friend Mrs Carter *could make a pudding as well as translate Epictetus* – but clearly the priority lay with the pudding.) Swift's sally would therefore be keenly appreciated by some of the company, the formally educated menfolk, leaving others baffled and smiling uncertainly, in the fashion of those who acknowledge a pleasantry without understanding it.

Interpreted thus, the joke begins to look a little too smart, too hard and shiny with wit's metallic gleam. We imagine the poor lady's embarrassment when the violin topples to the floor, and her deepening confusion when those educated men burst into a laughter of which she feels herself to be the cause, yet which she cannot in the least understand. Does no one comfort her? Does no one say, 'Never mind, these things happen, it shouldn't have been left there in the first place'? Swift's pun, clever as it is, seems to jibe round these simple humanities, to assert a conceited maleness in the face of the poor, ignorant, disaster-prone female. So, at all events, a story-teller might read the occurrence.

On the other hand, the conjunction of accident and comment might be construed in a quite different way. Supposing the lady to be greatly distressed, and the violin to be dismayingly valuable, we might read into Swift's joke a kindly attempt to ease the burden of the event by distracting attention from it. This is surely as plausible as any other account of the matter. Then what was the truth about Swift's witticism? Did it merely illustrate the nervous necessity of joking, an affliction as stubborn as a stutter? Was it the compulsion of a clever man to draw attention to himself? Was it a way of laying claim – he being a humble domestic chaplain, there among the wealthy and well-born at that Dublin Castle entertainment – to a certain authority and intellectual rank? Was it a useful device for smoothing out an unluckily wrinkled moment? Biography does not tell us. In one way or another, however, the clever citation from Virgil had a social intent, taking a certain situation into scope and exercising control over it. To make an allusion is often to make a bid for situational power, the kind of power that interprets, comments, directs responses and allots social roles.

5.2 THE CONTENT ELEMENT

Swift asked of his hearers something more than the recognition of a familiar piece of text. They were to be men of letters, certainly; but they were also to be ordinary social beings with an eye to worldly things, aware that *Mantua* was the name for that sort of gown, knowing that the best violins were made in Cremona. Clearly, this material/social content of the allusion is every whit as important as the citation that frames it; for Swift's purposes, what worse ignoramus might there be than the scholar who could translate the Latin yet still not see the joke, because dressmaking and musical instruments were beyond his interest? To live with the witty it is not enough to be literate; one must also be socially competent.

Most allusions make some demand on our competence as social beings with ready access to certain facts and commonplaces; when we lack such access, the allusion misfires, and becomes material for expository comment. Consider, for example, this *graffito*, quoted in an earlier chapter: *Harwich for the continent, Frinton for the incontinent*. This is a joke so exclusive as to be (perhaps) barely intelligible outside East Anglia, where it originated, and it is very largely the 'socio-cultural' content of the witticism that makes it obscure. The language is English, but there will be many English speakers for whom it might as well be Latin.

There are three important facts: (a) that Harwich, a small port on the east coast of England, is the point of departure for ferry services to Holland, (b) that road signs in the vicinity announce 'Harwich for the Continent', and (c) that the small resort of Frinton, not far from Harwich, has a population that includes many elderly and retired people. In an explanation of the joke these circumstances would have to be made clear, for the benefit even of native speakers of English. For those whose native language is not English, it would perhaps be necessary to add a linguistic commentary on the textual locus of the allusion, the counterpointing of the noun *continent* (= 'large land mass') and the adjective *incontinent* (= 'unable to control the urinary function'). Such explanation inevitably destroys the joke; things that are allusively funny lose their humorous charm when classification sets in.

5.3 THE LINGUISTIC ELEMENT

Failure to appreciate the 'content element' undermines the allusive joke. Equally, the humorous effect must lapse if the textual form of the allusion goes unrecognized, or is misunderstood in its peculiar relationship to the content. Thus, to grasp Swift's joke fully, we must (a) be able to recognize and translate a quotation from Virgil, and (b) understand that the words *nimium vicina*, in their humorous application, have the meaning not of *proximity* but of *physical contact*. (So a drunk may explain his black eye by saying that the lamppost came too close to his face.) This is another level of appeal; the jester invites the listener/reader to rejoice in his own literary and linguistic knowledge.

Many allusions turn on quotations from literary works:

Languid recruit: 'Now more than ever seems it rich to die'.
Ferocious drill sergeant: 'WHO SAID THAT!?'
Languid recruit: 'Keats, wasn't it?'

The languid one controls this situation with a quotation and a twist in the entailment of a question; asked, in effect, 'Who spoke?', he answers the query 'Who was the author of that line?' The basis of his momentary power is that the drill sergeant is excluded from the number of those who might be expected to recognize the allusion. This exclusiveness is a common characteristic of the literary joke.

It defines a group of adept insiders, and in doing so confirms feelings of privilege, not to say of superiority.

In an allusion, however, the cited text need not be from a poem or any other recognized piece of literature. Virtually any well known form of words – from the language of politics, of advertising, or journalism, of law and social administration – will serve the requirements of wit. A music critic, reviewing a performance of Bruch's violin concerto, notes the unusually slow tempi adopted by the soloist, Shlomo Mintz; and jocosely adds his supposition that this violinist is 'one of the too-good-to-hurry Mintz'. British readers can laugh at this, because they will almost certainly recognize the allusion to an advertising jingle no longer in use but popular in its day:

Murraymints, Murraymints,
Too-good-to-hurry mints.

The allusion is impudently funny, and at the same time makes a criticism that might have been more woundingly phrased; the reviewer does not use expressions like 'cloying', or 'self-indulgent', but something of the kind may be implied in his quip. Once again, we can regard the allusion as a controlling element in discourse; here, its effect is both to direct and to deflect the severity of criticism.

Another property of the textual component in allusion is that it may echo or mimic, rather than make a literal citation, and thus become a kind of minimal parody. A BBC/TV comedy series called *Sorry*! has an episode with a nice example of the parodic allusion. The hero, an ineffectual, undersized, endlessly-harassed and mother-bothered librarian, is attempting to persuade a brawny and aggressive refuse-collector to accept an illicitly-deposited bag of rubbish. The dustman snarls his rejection, proclaiming, as he looms menacingly over the librarian, that 'a bag is a bag is a bag'. Here the script-writer is playing a game of pleasant complication. He assumes, in the first place, that at least some of his TV audience will identify the mimicry of Gertrude Stein's 'a rose is a rose is a rose'. Should others unluckily miss the allusion, they may still be satisfied by the visual comedy and the general absurdity of the situation. Secondly, he puts the literary reference into the mouth of the dustman, a visibly non-literary character. This is charmingly incongruous (a sort of Alfred Doolittle joke); furthermore, it decisively allots to the dustman the control of the situation and the victory in the conflict. His retributory muscle is not physical but verbal; he beats down the opposition with the opposition's own weapons.

5.4 ALLUSION AND THE STRUCTURE OF TEXTS

Humorous allusions can evidently be used to control situations and condition attitudes – to smooth over a difficulty, to ward off an attack, to help the underdogged against the overbearing, to comment on society and manners. The example of the literary dustman, however, suggests another way in which the allusion has a controlling power. It can enter into the patterning of literary texts, and thus become one of the keys or signposts to interpretation with which those texts are furnished.

Elsewhere (in §2.6) we have considered the role of allusion in the making of a poem, Philip Larkin's *I Remember, I Remember*. Let us now examine a novelist's use of the key allusive phrase, taking a small instance from Keith Waterhouse's *Billy Liar*. This book tells the story of Billy Fisher (the 'Billy Liar' of the title), a young man whose daydreams and fantasies direct his life and distort his moral perceptions. Billy inhabits a world of images derived from films, romantic literature, and popular entertainments. Only his friend Arthur is able in some measure to understand and share Billy's inventive fantasies, upon which the dialogue of their friendship largely depends. At times, however, even Arthur is dismayed by Billy's obsessive devotion to falsehood:

> 'No, look seriously though, you haven't said our old woman's broken her leg, have you?' said Arthur.
> 'Course I have.'
> 'She'll go bloody bald, man! What if I'd called at your house and your old woman had asked after her?'
> 'You would have risen to the occasion,' I said, mock-heroically.
> 'The liefulness is terrific,' said Arthur, entering reluctantly into the mood of banter. [32; *p* 45]

The two speech-reporting expressions, *mock-heroically* and *entering reluctantly into the mood of banter*, are of importance to the design of the narrative. They signal the switch from 'real' conversation, dealing with acts and consequences, to a fantasy language of 'literary' postures and fictitious roles. When real life comes too close to Billy, requiring him to answer awkward questions, he makes these shifts into the mock-heroic, or the mock-romantic, or the merely mocking.

Arthur is obliged to accept the shift on this occasion, and he signals his reluctant acceptance with a mock-quotation ('the liefulness is terrific') in the style of Hurree Jam Singh, one of the pupils at Greyfriars School in the 'Billy Bunter' stories of Frank Richards. The allusion to a popular serial in a boys' magazine (where all occasions are risen to, and all happy or heroic roles are played) is presumably Arthur's way of indicating that he recognizes the evasive stratagem called by Billy 'the mood of banter'; the mock-literary statement (*You would have risen to the occasion*) elicits the mock-literary response. At the same time, it is possible to read a reproof into Arthur's words. Into his allusion is coded a troubled suggestion of puerility, though Billy is too self-absorbed to read the code.

The 'Greyfriars' allusion occurs again, in a scene which shows Billy acting out a fantasy of courtship and presenting to one Rita, a snack-bar waitress, a piece of jewellery that is not his to give. He is apparently unaware of the possibility that his action may hurt and deceive; he despises Rita, seeing her as sexually attractive but coarse-grained, and refuses to accept her clumsy pleasure in his gift and its implications:

> Rita picked up my empty plate, a move I recognized as an obscure gesture of affection. 'You can bring me a fur coat tomorrer,' she said genially. She went back to the counter, leaving us sitting at the rockety table in the corner of the Kit Kat by the huge, throbbing refrigerator.
>
> 'The sexfulness is terrific', Arthur said, watching her go. [32; *p* 103]

Here again, the allusion will bear a dual reading, as a token of Arthur's complicity in Billy's fantasizing, and also as a wry comment on the emptiness of a 'relationship' which (like the *huge, throbbing refrigerator*) makes a suggestive noise but lacks warmth.

5.5 ALLUSION INTO PARODY

Thus allusion can be an important, indeed cardinal, device in the structure of comic texts. Furthermore, wherever allusions occur some excursion into parody is possible; the parodic line often begins with the allusive point. Once more, *Billy Liar* provides an illustration. Arthur's allusive words, quoted above, prompt a typical response from Billy. He immediately goes into one of his 'routines' (his own word), a parody of music-hall patter rendered into pseudo-Biblical idiom:

> 'Lo, she is the handmaiden of my desires!' I said, raising a solemn right hand. Arthur took the cue to go into the Bible routine.
>
> 'And a voice spake,' he said in a loud, quavering voice. 'And the voice said Lo, who was that lady I saw ye with last cock-crow?'
>
> 'And Moses girded up his loins and said Verily, that was no lady, that was my spouse,' I responded.
>
> 'Yea, and it was so.'
>
> 'Yea, even unto the fifth and sixth generations.' We finished our coffee and got up, guffawing and blowing kisses at Rita. 'Don't do owt I wouldn't do!' she called, in an unusual mood herself. [32; *pp* 103–4]

Billy's parodic 'routine' alludes, by way of content, to a well-worn joke:

> 'Who was that lady I saw you with last night?'
>
> – 'That was no lady, that was my wife.'

The allusion provides a lumpish theme for clumsy parodic variations in a style based on recollections of Biblical phraseology. Recollection – perhaps one might say *organized* recollection – is fundamental to parody, and the act of recollecting is the act of alluding to actual or typical turns of phrase; thus Billy's *even unto the fifth and sixth generations* may be his vague recollection of a phrase in the second Commandment, *even unto the third and fourth generation*, while the 'girding up' of 'loins' is an Old Testament commonplace – *eg* in I Kings, xviii, 46, *He girded up his loins and ran before Ahab*.

Billy's parodies are part of Billy's general act of lying. Throughout the book he speaks dismissively of other people's attempts at humour, and clearly regards himself as a wit (one of his ambitions is to write comedy scripts); but his 'routines' are callow and self-indulgent. Through them, as through some cheap stimulant, he escapes from the puzzlement, inconvenience, and pain of everyday relationships, ordinary crises, honest promises, real work. Arthur's allusive remark, *the sexfulness is terrific*, gives Billy licence to forget Rita's flawed and fumbling humanity. She dwindles into mere suggestive syllables. She ceases to be a human being with desires and aspirations; she becomes a 'handmaiden' with 'sexfulness', an object for word-play. Because he is unable to meet the obligations of a reality unadorned by the flattering word and the consoling image, Billy Fisher thinks, speaks, and acts parodically, in *styles* that make life amusing and acceptable.

The notion of presenting character as a parodic tissue is of course not unique to *Billy Liar*; it is one of the ways in which the parodic process and parodic styles may enter into the structure of comic narrative. When we observe these effects, however, we are witnessing a particular use of parody, without, perhaps, learning much about how parodies are made. For most people the word 'parody' does not suggest the sophistication of a narrative mode: it suggests a mocking or hostile imitation of a well-known piece of text, a style, or a body of opinions and beliefs. Granting at least that parody is, by its very nature, *imitative*, we are now confronted with the task of trying to explain the varieties and the mechanisms of the mimetic process.

5.6 PARODY AS APPRAISAL: (I): PERSONAL STYLES

Robert Graves sees an image of parody in the folk myth of the witch who invisibly stalks her victim, following close on his heels and imitating his gait so aptly that she at last possesses it, and can make him stumble at will. This striking comparison suggests that parody appraises – learns the way of walking – in order to ridicule and discomfit. But not all parody is hostile; many acts of literary caricature and burlesque show affectionate familiarity with the things they imitate, and are a form of positive criticism, of stylistic analysis, and ultimately of tribute. If there are malign witches, there are also benevolent warlocks, who learn the steps in order to show just how well the 'victim' dances. Parody of a personal style often aims to do just that. It is the shortest and most concrete way of commenting on typical features of syntax, lexicon, phonology, prosody, and all the apparatus of learned dissertation.

The point is illustrated by the following attempt, on my part, to parody the distinctive poetic idiom of Gerard Manley Hopkins:

G. M. HOPKINS TAKES LUNCH IN THE RESTAURANT CAR

Ah, waiter, are there any any, where are, tell me, come,
    Napkins, lovely all-of-a-starch-staring

Linen, preferably, or pauper-seeming paper, waiter? Wearing
 My gaygear goodsuit, ah, my dear, dim was it? dumb?
Well, this train's tripping and track-truckling as I sipped
 Soup, did, ah God, the hot of it! – yes, slipped, flipped
Into my lap, slapping, of this clear consommé, some
 Spoonflung flashes, splashes for bosom's bearing.

Bring me a – coo – lummy – here dab, here dry with a kerch-
 ief, tea-towel, toilet-roll, oh-dear-then-a-doyly, but merely
A move (with a mercy, man) make! Oh what a slanting that
 sheerly,
 What with the canting curve of the, what with the lilt of the
 lurch,
Hurled leaping lapward, all in a skirl, the dear drenching.
 There was a splash to abash one quaintly, ah, there was a
 quenching!
Since when, on seat's edge sodden I pensive perch,
 Picking at lunch unlovely, unappetizing nearly.

The intention of this light-hearted exercise is certainly not to stage a satirical attack on a sage and serious poet. The parody aims affectionately at the comprehension of certain stylistic mannerisms, and it is the parodist who is at risk here, should the purport of his mimetic tricks go unrecognized. To say what these 'tricks' are, and how they reflect the devices habitually used by the poet, is to embark on a primary course in Hopkinsian poetics. Here are the familiar prosodic and phonetic idiosyncrasies, the 'sprung rhythm' with its jostling clusters of strong accents, the linking alliterations and assonances, the internal rhyming, the 'rove over' rhyme (*with a kerch/ief, tea towel*: *etc*). Here also are the characteristic syntactic patterns: the interrupted constructions, the parentheses, the ellipses, the bold departures from normal word order, the phrasal modifiers, the liking for certain phrase types (*eg* the 'of-genitive', *the X of Y*, and the 's-genitive' with participial noun, *the Y's Xing*. 'The vocabulary, too, clearly purports to represent Hopkins' lexical preoccupations – the abundant compounds and phrasal adjectives, the deviant semantics (as in 'the *lilt* of the lurch', 'all in a *skirl*'), the liking for words suggesting rapid and violent action or motion (*hurl* is a favourite).

The validity of these brief analytical notes can be tested against the poet's work. Anyone interested enough to make the test might possibly mark in passing some apparently direct verbal borrowings from Hopkins' poems, or perhaps some general resemblances of phraseology between the parody and the original corpus. Although these correspondences were not consciously sought when the parody was made, memory has indeed been at its sneaking craft, as a few examples may show:

Hopkins: 'How to keep – is there any any, is there none such, nowhere known some, bow or brooch . . .'
(The Leaden Echo and The Golden Echo)

Parody: 'Ah, waiter, are there any, any, where are, tell me, come, Napkins . . .'

Hopkins: '. . . to-fro tender trambeams truckle at the eye'
(*The Candle Indoors*)

Parody: 'This train's tripping and track-truckling . . .'

Hopkins: 'But how shall I . . . make me a room there:
Reach me a . . . Fancy, come faster –'
(*The Wreck of the Deutschland*)

Parody: 'Bring me a – coo – lummy – here dab, here dry . . .'

Hopkins: 'The girth of it and the wharf of it . . .'
(*The Wreck of the Deutschland*)

Parody: '. . . the hot of it'

Hopkins: '. . . and blue-beak embers, ah my dear, Fall . . .'
(*The Windhover*)

Parody: My gaygear goodsuit, ah, my dear, dim was it . . .?

Such echoes, however, are ultimately of minor interest and are perhaps irrelevant to the question of whether or not the parody is effective. A test of good parody is not how closely it imitates or reproduces certain turns of phrase, but how well it *generates* a style convincingly like that of the parodied author, producing the sort of phrases and sentences he might have produced. Borrowing the terminology of language acquisition, we might say that the parodist displays a competence, learns to 'speak Hopkins' and to produce Hopkinsian utterances which he has never heard before.

Something, therefore, is *added* to an effective and interesting parody; it is not solely or even primarily an exercise in specific allusion to certain textual loci, but an attempt at a *creative allusiveness* that generates the designated style. To this, add one further element: the intrusion of the parodist's own idiom, or at all events of a patently alien accent (*dim was it*? *dumb*?; *coo – lummy* –) confessing to the irreverent act, reminding the reader, should he need reminding, that this is not the style itself, not a blatant forgery, not an attempt to pass off as genuine a gobbet of pastiche, but something that remains from first to last a piece of jocose mimicry. The apparent ineptitudes of the clown are at one and the same time the setting for his burlesque act and his admission that it *is* a burlesque and nothing more.

5.7 PARODY AS APPRAISAL: (II) THE HOSTILE STANCE

In some cases, however, the burlesque has sardonic overtones; the clown's eye glitters, the parodist's voice develops a rasp. When parody is the vehicle for hostile criticism, it may be aimed at a pretentiously mannered style (this is the case with the many cockshies at Poe's *The Raven*), or, more often, it may attack a content *through* a style. Parody and satire are not the same thing, but parody becomes a satirical weapon when the parodist is angered by an author's philosophies, arguments, or recurrent attitudes. Here is a burlesque of D. H. Lawrence's verse style, written by me in a mood of reaction against Lawrence's moralistic bullying. It might qualify for the description 'satirical parody':

BERT LAWRENCE GETS THE BUG

I saw a bug today,
in the quadrangle, as a matter of fact;
and that's how he looked, all matter-of-fact
and bug-like, in the way of bugs.

I was mooching along with my head down,
as people do mooch along with their heads down,
and I saw him, my bug,
I did, I did, I saw him,
there!
In the vast expanse of the quadrangle,
waiting.

Oh and instantly I took to him,
I did, I liked him, I fell in love with him, I could have kissed

him as an Indian kisses his squaw, with a lovely drawn-out kiss, taking his time about it,
and truly I could have gone down on my hunkers and cuddled him, grappled with him,
grappling and cuddling like a very close acquaintance,
because he was complete, very bug of very bug;
lovely!

He was bug-like as no man is ever man-like,
so intensely a bug, so true to the bug-force within himself.
Ah!
I watched him sprattle
as bugs do sprattle,
with their legs like so, like bugs' legs, stretched out and sprattling.
and I thought good for you, bug,
none of these abominable tricks for you.

None of this whining about the state of the world,
none of this disgusting pity,
this corrosive canting doctrine of compassion.
Errgggh!

That's what's wrong with people nowadays,
always snivelling and weeping for somebody,
always sorry for something,
with their rotten compassion like a fungus in them.
Rotten beggars!

That is not your way, bug,
You don't lie there waiting for someone to feel sorry for you,
you sprattle with all the bug-gladness in your bug-heart,
you do, you sprattle.

Oh, and I liked him, I could have got down and shaken him by the hand,
if bugs have hands,
twining man-hand into bug-hand, patiently and carefully, as the Arapaho women weave blankets for the best bed in the wigwam, totally absorbed in their task, absorbed and waiting for their man to come home and say never mind your blanket, scrub my back.

I could have done something of the sort.
But instead I stamped on him and squelched him into a
squiggle, right there in the vast expanse of the quadrangle,
squiggled him into a squelch, squashed the life out of him
with my boot,
raising and lowering my foot rhythmically, once, twice, three
times.
And don't think I felt sorry for him, because I didn't.
That is not my way.

This invites general observations of the kind already made about our Hopkins parody. Any reader of Lawrence will detect allusive sources in his poems about animals (*eg*: *Snake*) or in the verses written during his New Mexico days (the work-absorbed women being, of course, the Navajo, not the Arapaho). It must be clear, however, that this is not simply a piece of stylistic fun, let alone an admiring tribute. There is angry impatience in the poem, impatience at Lawrentian attitudes, and it expresses itself most powerfully where the allusive/parodic grasp is at its weakest:

None of this whining about the state of the world,
none of this disgusting pity,
this corrosive canting doctrine of compassion.
Errgggh!

In these lines, a tetchy irony appears to take over from the kind of parody that shrewdly studies its target-language and makes telling inventions of typical phrases. Lawrence's ideas are attacked, but the stylistic routing of the attack is for the moment not wholly apparent. The reader may take it for granted that there is a parodic intention, and may indeed detect in this passage an echo of the hectoring and scornful accents of Lawrence at his polemic worst; but the voucher of parody is not so plain that if the lines were presented in isolation they would immediately proclaim 'Lawrence', or even 'an imitation of someone's style'.

5.8 THE RECOGNITION OF PARODY

There arises the question of how we recognize a parody or a parodic intention; for here, as in other forms of humour, laughter depends on some framework of expectancy. Most commonly, as in our Hopkins parody, a title makes the directive signal, even suggesting the structure of the parodic joke. The reader is given some form of stylistic proposition; a poet's name is mentioned, and a content (*eg*: *lunch in the restaurant car*) is indicated. Thus he is led to presuppose a model of this type:

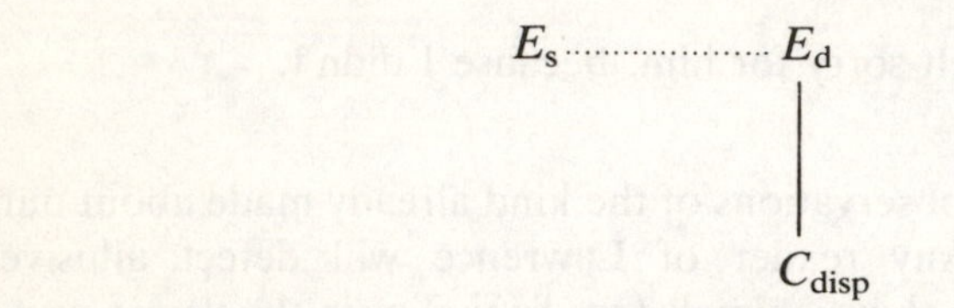

This represents two 'planes', of *expression* and *content*. E_s is the source-expression (*eg* Hopkins' style as observed in his poems), from which the parodic expression E_d is *derived*. The content of the parody is totally unHopkinsian; his usual subject-matter has been *displaced*, so to speak, by an untypical theme. Hence, E_d = 'derived expression', and C_{disp} = 'displacing content'.

The presuppositions encouraged by the title are confirmed, or at any rate tested, by the ensuing text; as we have seen, the E_d may pick up identifiable scraps from the E_s or, more broadly, may generate a phraseology suggestive of the E_s. If the parody is successful, the model-proposing title is strictly speaking unnecessary; nevertheless, it has a part to play, in orientating the reader. Were there no title, or were the title less explicit (*eg*: *Eminent Victorian in Hot Water*), he would have to make his own guess at the intended style. There would be an implied query – 'Guess who?' – which would turn the exercise from a humorous demonstration into a riddle or charade. The title, then, is part of a conditioning process that lets the reader in on the joke.

Yet in the absence of a title, even when the reader is not sure just what is being parodied, it may still be possible to recognize parodic intention. The parodist takes care as a rule to create notable discrepancies: discrepancies of 'fit' between expression and content, and discrepancies of style on the plane of expression itself. In the Hopkins parody, the mismatch of expression and content is boldly obvious, and must be so even to a reader with no knowledge of Hopkins. 'Cry like this over spilt soup?' he asks himself. 'This has to be a joke.' Similarly, he must have his doubts about the seriousness of a rhetoric that veers abruptly from the pseudo-poetic (*eg*: *bosom's bearing*) to the banally coloquial (*coo – lummy –*). Perception of stylistic discrepancy confirms his assumptions about the wayward content; what he has before him is either a piece of absurdly ill-judged writing, or an essay in buffoonery, *probably* of a parodic nature.

Why that cautious qualifier, *probably*? It is because humorous writing may have a parodic semblance without being a parody of anything in particular, and because we can hugely enjoy a text without being able to identify a parodic source. Consider the following passage. Is it a parody, with a source in the work of a particular author, or is it merely an enjoyably absurd piece of literary spoof?

> It needed but a glance at the new-comer to detect at once the form and features of the haughty aborigine – the untaught and untrammelled son of the forest. Over one shoulder a blanket, negligently but gracefully thrown, disclosed a bare and powerful breast, decorated with a quantity of three-cent postage-stamps which he had despoiled from an Overland Mail stage a few weeks previously. A cast-off beaver of Judge Tompkins's, adorned by a simple feather, covered his erect head, from beneath which his straight locks descended. His right hand hung lightly by his side, while his left was engaged in holding on a pair of pantaloons, which the lawless grace and freedom of his lower limbs evidently could not brook.
>
> 'Why,' said the Indian, in a low sweet tone, – 'why does the Pale Face still follow the track of the Red Man? Why does he pursue him, even as *O-kee-chow*, the wild-cat, chases *Ka-ka*, the skunk? Why are the feet of *Sorrel-top*, the white chief, among the acorns of *Muck-a-Muck*, the mountain forest? Why,' he repeated, quietly but firmly abstracting a silver spoon from the table, – 'why do you seek to drive him from the wigwams of his fathers? His brothers are already gone to the happy hunting-grounds. Will the Pale Face seek him there?' And, averting his face from the Judge, he hastily slipped a silver cake-basket beneath his blanket, to conceal his emotion.
>
> '*Muck-a-Muck* has spoken,' said Genevra, softly. 'Let him now listen. Are the acorns of the mountain sweeter than the esculent and nutritious bean of the Pale Face miner? Does my

brother prize the edible qualities of the snail above that of the crisp and oleaginous bacon? Delicious are the grasshoppers that sport on the hillside – are they better than the dried apples of the Pale Faces? Pleasant is the gurgle of the torrent, Kish-Kish, but is it better than the cluck-cluck of old Bourbon from the old stone bottle?'

'Ugh!' said the Indian, – 'ugh! good. The White Rabbit is wise. Her words fall as the snow on Tootoonolo, and the rocky heart of Muck-a-Muck is hidden. What says my brother the Gray Gopher of Dutch Flat?

'She has spoken, Muck-a-Muck,' said the Judge, gazing fondly on his daughter. 'It is well. Our treaty is concluded. No, thank you, – you need *not* dance the Dance of Snow Shoes, or the Moccasin Dance, the Dance of Green Corn, or the Treaty Dance. I would be alone. A strange sadness overpowers me.'

'I go,' said the Indian. 'Tell your great chief in Washington, the Sachem Andy, that the Red Man is retiring before the footsteps of the adventurous Pioneer. Inform him, if you please, that westward the star of empire takes its way, that the chiefs of the Pi-Ute nation are for Reconstruction to a man, and that Klamath will poll a heavy Republican vote in the fall.'

And folding his blanket more tightly about him, Muck-a-Muck withdrew.
[15; p 339*ff*]

The first thing to acknowledge about this is that it is funny. Joyless must that reader be who can sit unsmiling while Muck-a-Muck, noble scion of nature, hitches his pants and snitches the silverware – *quietly but firmly*, like the aristocrat he is; or who can harden his features against Genevra's mirthfully magniloquent discourse on such benefits of civilization as *the esculent and nutritious bean* and *the cluck-cluck of old Bourbon from the old stone bottle*. The piece is certainly funny enough in its own right to survive without the supporting reference of a parodied original. Yet a reader with any sense of literary conventions must surely suspect parody. Something is being mocked here. It is a familiar scene, this tableau of the simple Red Man coming to pow-wow with his white brother, who sympathizes with the sons of the wild, yet knows (with a strange sadness) that the march of the future cannot be halted. Very familiar it is –

for lo, have we not seen it shining on the Great White Cloth of *Kine-ma*, where the braves bite on *Chok-ba* and *Pop-kon*, crying *yay*? Never before, however, have we witnessed such devious urbanity in the Pale Faces (their log cabin is appointed within like a *salon*, with a grand piano and pictures by Tintoretto and Rubens), or such scruffy delinquency in the clean-limbed prince of the prairie; and certainly we have never heard the Indian chief make remarkable switches of rhetoric, from Simple Savage (*ugh*!) to Basic Civil Servant (*Inform him, if you please*), from Redmanspeak (*the rocky heart of Muck-a-Muck is hidden*) to Hustingtalk (*westward the star of empire makes its way . . . will poll a heavy Republican vote in the fall*). There are hilarious discrepancies, in the style and the handling of the content; discrepancies of the kind that characterize the parodic method.

And it is indeed a parody – by Bret Harte, of Fenimore Cooper's *Leatherstocking* novels (an iconographic source, incidentally, for many a matinée Western). The object of Harte's mockery is not solely Cooper's extraordinary narrative style. The Cooper content (take one rude man of the woods, add one gently-nurtured female, and whisk to a paste) also comes under attack. Here, as in one of our earlier examples, the parody of D. H. Lawrence, assault on content is bound up with mimicry of style. We may contrast 'style parody', as in the Hopkins example, with 'style-and-content' parody, the latter being modelled thus;

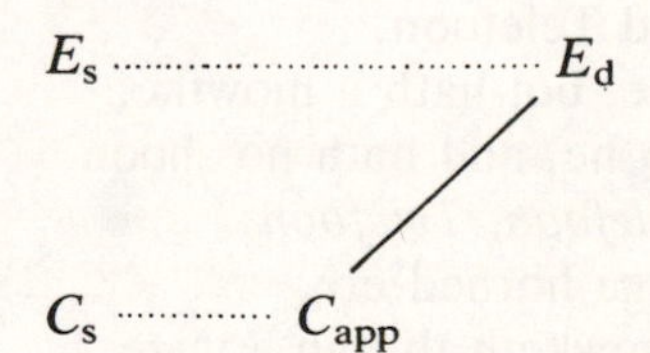

On the content plane there is a source-content (*eg* the poems of Lawrence, the novels of Fenimore Cooper), which yields to an *apposed* content, *ie* a theme resembling, or plausibly comparable with, or at least not generically different from, those of the source material. Cooper does write about Rousseauesque roughnecks and salon sophisticates; Lawrence may not write about bugs specifically, but he has given us poems lauding the endowments of the snake, the tortoise, the lizard, the mosquito, *etc*, themes to which a further bit of zoological moralizing is quite apposite. 'He *might* have chosen this subject', says the parodist to the reader. Not all parodies written in this way are unfriendly, but still a fairly common mode of parodic attack is to father a likely subject onto the victim, and then bring out its absurdity with an irreverent simulation of his style.

5.9 THE PARODY OF PERIOD STYLES

The recognition of a parody may be difficult if the target is an author or a particular work unknown to the reader. There is so much that we have not read; the poems, the novels, pass us by and are lost to our experience. Out of these artefacts, however, out of the continued practice of writing from generation to generation, there arises something we call 'literary language', representing the stylistic character of whole periods in our culture – 'mediaeval', 'Elizabethan', Restoration', *etc.* The teacher of literature assumes that his pupils will have some feeling, some rough-and-ready sense of period styles, and will carry in their heads, for reference purposes, a broad image of the language of the fourteenth or sixteenth or seventeenth centuries. Dependence on a recognition of 'the sort of thing I mean' underlies parodies such as this, my response to the mediaeval genre of the riddle-poem:

TELEFOON

Ther ys one wight I fere, y-wis,
He ys y-cleped Telefoon.
He hath no hede, bot hath a mowthe,
One fote hath he, and hath no shoon,
Telefoon, Telefoon
He hath one huge horned ere,
Hys fode he sowketh thurgh a wyre.
Telefoon no moder hath,
Bel ys Telefoones syre,
Telefoon, Telefoon
Whenne he hereth *Belles* voys
He rejoyseth, answerynge
Wyth a noyse repetitif,
Wyth a selie tynge-a-lynge,
Telefoon, Telefoon
On hys breste he bereth a whele
Wyth nombres magycke rownde the rym;

Nombres summonen hys frendes,
  Thei wyth ryngynge answeren hym,
    Telefoon, Telefoon
Nyl I nat approchen hym
  Bot wyth grucchynge and wyth grone.
Telefoon ys mannes foo,
  I wol leven hym allone,
    Telefoon, Telefoon

This is on the face of it a particular token of the general type of 'style parody':

E_s .... E_d
|
C_{disp}

Whether the telephone-theme is wholly a 'displacing content' is, however, a matter that invites some reflection. The general principles of the parody are clear. Firstly, we note that the E_s is not the style of a particular author, but of a period and a genre; the 'lyric' may consequently be read as a happy-go-lucky hit at the language and conventions of Middle English. It is hardly necessary to be a philologist in order to read it, and indeed the writer of such a piece must take care *not* to philologize very strictly, or the discrepancies of expression that give the joke its force will be lost. There is a presumption, however, that the reader will have come across something, perhaps some text in his school curriculum, the recollection of which will serve him here. The E_d, the derived expression, is not so much Middle as Muddle English – a macaronic medley of words ancient and modern. The essential parodic mismatchings are here; the very title exhibits a kind of discrepancy, in its realignment of a familiar reference (the telephone) with an unfamiliar spelling and the implication of an unfamiliar pronunciation.

The title has, in fact, a dual reference, which may lead us to reconsider our initial labelling of the theme as a 'displacing content':

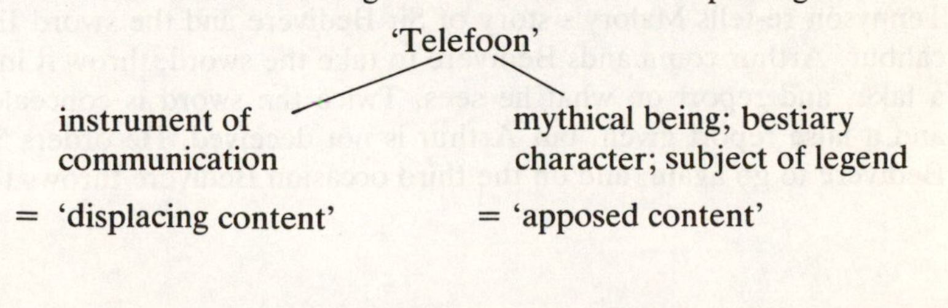

Such duality typifies the myth-making which is often a concomitant of parody. For the humour of the myth to take effect, the reader must accept both references, bearing in mind the characteristics and components of the telephone instrument while he assembles the image of the Telefoon-beast. Then a playful creativity can go to work with puns and allusions: '*Bel* ys Telefoones syre' suggests (a) a curiously-endowed god from some heathen pantheon, (b) the name of Alexander Graham Bell, or of the Bell Telephone Company, and (c) the telephone bell itself. The imagination plays with the interacting and apparently discrepant notions of the telephone as instrument and as monster.

Another kind of parodic discrepancy, then – between a 'displacing content' (the modern device, mechanical and unmysterious) and an 'apposed content' (the riddling, myth-focusing emblem, just the sort of theme a mediaeval lyricist might have taken up). The *Telefoon* poem conjoins two parodic models:

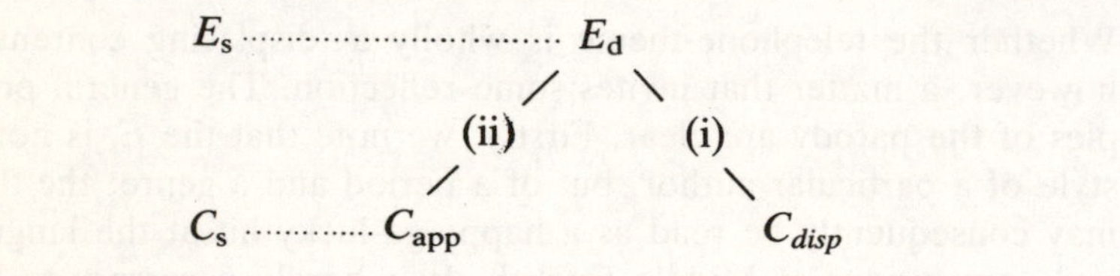

5.10 COMPLEX PARODIC SCHEMES

There are, indeed, many parodies that represent a conjoining of models. Parodic complexity is achieved when, for instance, the content of one text is mocked in a style imitative of another. J.C. Squire provides an amusing example in a piece called *If Lord Byron Had Written 'The Passing Of Arthur'* (it is one of a collection called *How They Would Have Done It*). To appreciate the parody, the reader must be acquainted with Byron's style in *Don Juan* – specifically, with the stanza form, the burlesque rhyming, the display of ironic banter. He must also be quite closely acquainted with *The Passing Of Arthur*, and in particular with that part of the poem in which Tennyson re-tells Malory's story of Sir Bedivere and the sword Excalibur. Arthur commands Bedivere to take the sword, throw it into a lake, and report on what he sees. Twice the sword is concealed and a false report given, but Arthur is not deceived. He orders Sir Bedivere to go again, and on the third occasion Bedivere throws the sword, sees an arm rise from the lake, catch the hilt, and draw it down beneath the water. Here is Tennyson describing Sir Bedivere's first false report, and his thoughts as he goes to the lake for a second time;

> Then spake King Arthur to Sir Bedivere:
> 'Hast thou performed my mission which I gave?
> What is it thou hast seen? or what hast heard?'
>
> And answer made the bold Sir Bedivere:
> 'I heard the ripple washing in the reeds,
> And the wild water lapping on the crag.'
>
> To whom replied King Arthur, faint and pale:
> 'Thou hast betrayed thy nature and thy name,
> Not rendering true answer, as beseemed
> Thy fealty, nor like a noble knight:
> For surer sign had followed, either hand,
> Or voice, or else a motion of the mere.
> This is a shameful thing for men to lie.
> Yet now, I charge thee, quickly go again,
> As thou art lief and dear, and do the thing
> I bade thee, watch, and lightly bring me word.'
>
> Then went Sir Bedivere the second time
> Across the ridge, and paced beside the mere,
> Counting the dewy pebbles, fixed in thought;
> But when he saw the wonder of the hilt,
> How curiously and strangely chased, he smote
> His palms together, and he cried aloud:
>
> 'And if indeed I cast the brand away,
> Surely a precious thing, one worthy note,
> Should thus be lost for ever from the earth,
> Which might have pleased the eyes of many men.
> What good should follow this, if this were done?
> What harm, undone? Deep harm to disobey,
> Seeing obedience is the bond of rule.
> Were it well to obey then, if a king demand
> An act unprofitable, against himself?
> The King is sick, and knows not what he does.
> What record, or what relic of my lord
> Should be to aftertime, but empty breath

And rumours of a doubt? But were this kept,
Stored in some treasure-house of mighty kings,
Some one might show it at a joust of arms,
Saying "King Arthur's sword, Excalibur,
Wrought by the lonely maiden of the Lake.
Nine years she wrought it, sitting in the deeps
Upon the hidden bases of the hills."
So might some old man speak in the aftertime
To all the people, winning reverence.
But now much honour and much fame were lost.'

So spake he, clouded with his own conceit,
And hid Excalibur the second time,
And so strode back slow to the wounded King.

Then spoke King Arthur, breathing heavily:
'What is it thou hast seen? or what hast heard?'

And answer made the bold Sir Bedivere:
'I heard the water lapping on the crag,
And the long ripple washing in the reeds.'

To whom replied King Arthur, much in wrath:
'Ah, miserable and unkind, untrue,
Unknightly, traitor-hearted! Woe is me! . . .' [28; *p* 1748]

It is necessary to have in mind all the details of this episode – right down to Arthur's offended cry at the close – before we can begin to appreciate Squire's impudent Byronizing of Tennyson's epic narrative. The following stanzas parodically stalk the passage printed above:

So, having safely stowed away the sword
And marked the place with several large stones
Sir Bedivere returned to his liege lord
And, with a studious frankness in his tones,
Stated that he had dropped it overboard;
But Arthur only greeted him with groans:
'My Bedivere,' he said, 'I may be dying,
But even dead I'd spot such barefaced lying.

'It's rather rough upon a dying man
That his last dying orders should be flouted.

Time was when if you'd thus deranged my plan
  I should have said, "Regard yourself as outed,
I'll find some other gentleman who can."
  Now I must take what comes, that's all about it . . .
My strength is failing fast, it's very cold here.
Come, pull yourself together, be a soldier.

'Once more I must insist you are to lift
  Excalibur and hurl him in the mere.
Don't hang about now. You had better shift
  For all you're worth, or when you come back here
The chances are you'll find your master stiffed.'
  Whereat the agonized Sir Bedivere,
His 'Yes, Sire,' broken by a noisy sob,
Went off once more on his distasteful job.

But as he walked the inner voice did say:
  'I quite agree with "Render unto Caesar,"
But nothing's said of throwing things away
  When a man's king's an old delirious geezer,
You don't meet swords like this one every day.
  Jewels and filigree as fine as these are
Should surely be preserved in a museum
That our posterity may come and see 'em.

'A work of Art's a thing one holds in trust,
  One has no right to throw it in a lake,
Such Vandalism would arouse disgust
  In every Englishman who claims to take
An interest in Art. Oh, no, I must
  Delude my monarch for my country's sake;
Obedience in such a case, in fact,
Were patently an anti-social act.

'It is not pleasant to deceive my king,
  I had much rather humour his caprice,
But, if I tell him I have thrown the thing,
  And, thinking that the truth, he dies in peace,
Surely the poets of our race will sing
  (Unless they are the most pedantic geese)
The praises of the knight who lied to save
This precious weapon from a watery grave.'

He reached the margin of the lake and there
  Until a decent interval had passed
Lingered, the sword once more safe in its lair.
  Then to his anxious monarch hurried fast,
And, putting on a still more candid air,
  Assured the king the brand had gone at last.
But Arthur, not deceived by any means,
Icily said: 'Tell that to the marines.' [26; *p* 94]

We might enjoy the larkiness of this without knowing the source of Squire's parodic language; lines like *The chances are you'll find your master stiffed* and *When a man's king's an old delirious geezer* are funny as buffooning 'translations' of an original text (*The King is sick, and knows not what he does*) – funny enough, indeed, for a reader to enjoy the joke without having read a word of Byron. But obviously the humour is all the richer when we are able to recall the seriocomic situations, the style, the macaronic language of *Don Juan*, echoed here in the careless shifts from the literary to the colloquial, in the virtuosity of bad rhymes (*Caesar – geezer – these are*), in the brutally bland irony (*Oh, no, I must/Delude my monarch for my country's sake*) The parody is double-barrelled, aiming on the one hand at Byron's style, which is liable to degenerate into a set of jimdandy mannerisms, and on the other hand at Tennyson's content, in which the customary sublime is occasionally tempered by the gorblimey. There is a breezy irreverence, expressed through the pseudo-Byronic style, towards a classic piece of Victorian verse; and there is an implied criticism of the cheapjack facility of the Byronic verse-method. The model of this complex style-and-content parody may be set out as follows:

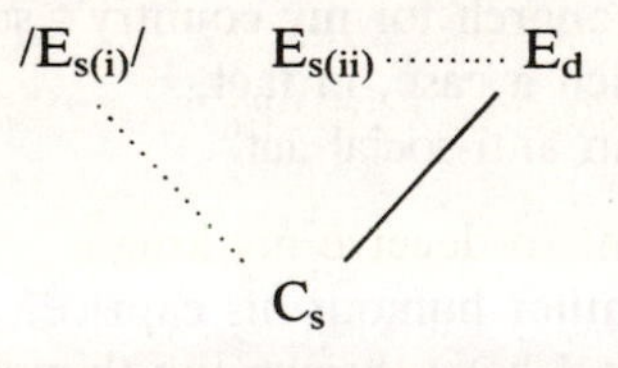

The source-content is that of Tennyson, in *The Passing of Arthur*; the source-expression is that of Byron's *Don Juan*, from which the parodic expression is derived. Note, however, that there are hints of Tennysonian language in the parody, in words like *brand* and *mere*, which, taken out of their epic context and put into clubmanchatty company (*Assured the king the brand had gone at last*) become comically quaint. The notation /$E_{s(i)}$/, indicating a source-expression (Tennyson's poetic language) that has been displaced, is thus not altogether accurate. Residual elements of this 'displaced' language *do* appear in the 'derived' parodic expression, and Squire's parody is therefore even more complicated than our diagrammatic model would suggest.

5.11 PSEUDOPARODY AND INTERTEXTUALITY

The domain of parody is, to be sure, a large and varied one – so much so, that we inevitably come across texts that are not centrally parodic, in terms of a clearly definable model, but which wear a parodic *aura*, and are full of echoes of half-remembered writings. They might be called *pseudoparodies*. Here is an example of pseudo-parody, produced during a tutorial on composition and creative writing, as an illustration of some rhetorical techniques:

> Milkmen everywhere. Milkmen up the Avenue; milkmen down the Grove. Milkmen on the High St, where it winds between banks of shops stacked with plastic footwear and cut-price washing machines; milkmen in the alleys that meander past the dirty backyards of dormant pubs. Milkmen rattling their bottles in areas and basements; milkmen wheedling incorrect sums from harassed housewives; milkmen with dejected horses; milkmen with electric floats, stuck at the traffic lights where the main road forks left past the grim grey majesty of the multi-storey car park.

The composition of this was haunted by the troubled sense of writing to a hidden model. Readers of the passage may have the impression of having met something like it elsewhere, and in their mental rummagings for a source may possibly remember the first page of Dickens' *Bleak House*:

> Fog everywhere. Fog up the river, where it flows among green aits and meadows; fog down the river, where it rolls defiled among the tiers of shipping, and the waterside pollutions of a great (and dirty) city. Fog on the Essex Marshes, fog on the Kentish heights. Fog creeping into the

> cabooses of collier-brigs; fog lying out on the yards, and hovering in the rigging of great ships; fog drooping on the gunwales of barges and small boats. Fog in the eyes and throats of ancient Greenwich pensioners, wheezing by the firesides of their wards; fog in the stem and bowl of the afternoon pipe of the wrathful skipper, down in his close cabin; fog cruelly pinching the toes and fingers of his shivering little 'prentice boy on deck. Chance people on the bridges peeping over the parapets into a nether sky of fog, with fog all round them, as if they were up in a balloon, and hanging in the misty clouds. [8]

Clearly, the 'milkman' exercise is an example of parodic recollection. It is not closely or pointedly imitative of the Dickens passage. If it were a deliberate and conscious parody, it would imitate the original's subtle variations of clause and sentence length, and its picture of a suburban High Street would offer some sort of iconographic parallel to the programme of the Dickensian Thames, which is followed from the meadows above London, through the city, and out to the estuary marshes. There is no conscious modelling of one passage on the other; but there is a hazy recollection of rhetorical procedures. We see, for instance, how the pseudoparody has picked up some linguistic features of its Dickensian original, *eg* the rarity of finite verbs, and the frequency of participle clauses and adverbial constructions. (Compare *Fog up the river, where it flows among green aits and meadows* with *Milkmen up the High St, where it winds between banks of shops: etc*; or *Fog creeping into the cabooses of collier-brigs* with *Milkmen rattling their bottles in areas and basements*.) These echoes suggest that a powerfully or idiosyncratically written passage, like the splendid opening of *Bleak House*, can lodge in a reader's mind a stylistic record for later reference.

This is one of the ways in which a literary language is created. The devices of some pattern-giving example are registered, as an ingenious mechanism of style; subsequent recollection – the pseudoparodic echo – turns the apparatus to other uses. There are cases of 'intertextuality' in which one text recalls another with commentary slyness; in other instances the sense of recollection is vaguer, and the writer appears to be imitating, in general, the kind of rhetoric appropriate to a convention or genre. Such pseudoparodic passages abound in comic writing; constantly, in reading comedy, we are aware of shifts in expression that mockingly shadow familiar features of style. In *Three Men In A Boat*, Jerome never tires of a game of stylistic deflation, in which the pretensions of pseudoparodic language are abruptly destroyed by banal comment. Sometimes he deceives his reader with paragraphs of orotund solemnity, abruptly dismissed with an urchin snigger. In other passages, the pseudoparodic element stands for one half of a comic dialogue. Jerome likes to play the role of straight man, and use his friend Harris as the knockabout:

> You can never rouse Harris. There is no poetry about Harris – no wild yearning for the unattainable. Harris never 'weeps, he knows not why'. If Harris's eyes fill with tears, you can bet it is because Harris has been eating raw onions, or has put too much Worcester sauce over his chop.
>
> If you were to stand at night by the seashore with Harris, and say:
>
> 'Hark! Do you not hear? Is it but the mermaids singing deep below the waving waters; or sad spirits, chanting dirges for white corpses, held by seaweed?'
>
> Harris would take you by the arm, and say:
>
> 'I know what it is, old man; you've got a chill. Now, you come along with me. I know a place round the corner here, where you can get a drop of the finest Scotch whisky you ever tasted – put you right in less than no time.' [17; *p* 18]

On Jerome's side of this interchange there is a literariness that appears not only in the direct quotation, but also in his phrasing generally. What is the origin of phrases like *wild yearning for the unattainable* and *sad spirits, chanting dirges for white corpses*? They sound like quotations, but they are not. They are surely *pseudoparodic*, of romantic rhetoric in general, with no reference to a specific text. So read, they characterize Jerome's studiously elegant clown-posture, which is countered by the *buffo* of Harris – *I know what it is, old man; you've got a chill.*

Elements of parody are so important in the style of comedy that the creation of a parodic texture may sometimes appear to be the exclusive principle of any comic work: Jerome is parodic, Bret Harte is parodic, Leacock is parodic, Thurber is parodic, novelists like Dickens and Evelyn Waugh are at least intermittently parodic, modern playwrights like Tom Stoppard and Joe Orton are parodic. One might certainly argue that one of the *axes* of comic writing – the 'style-axis', if we like to call it that – is a progression of allusions, parodic hints, pseudoparodies. There is, however, another principle, working in correlation with the devices of an echoic style: a principle of logic, or *logic-in-likelihood*. The comedian frequently shifts the ground of probability and subverts the rules of argument, and is able to do this very often with the help of a parodic style. Parody accommodates and even excuses the mockery of logic; the unlikely circumstance is made acceptable by the amusing distortions of parodic expression. Parodic style and subverted logic together define one essential quality of comic narrative; the integrity of its artifice – the 'artefactuality', to coin a monstrous word, that leads us to consider it purely in its own terms, as something distanced from all that is involved in the word *realism*. This may appear to be a paradoxical conclusion, since humour and comedy often have reference to social institutions and interactions, and are therefore commonly supposed to be realistic. They may be *truthful* in their reflections on human nature, but *realistic* is seldom the word for their style and narrative method. At their funniest, their wisest, their most revelatory, they transcend realism and require us to acquiesce in the laws of the surreal.

Six

Likelihoods and logics

6.1 A LIKELY TALE: 'ANYTHING CAN HAPPEN'

In hot pursuit of the canary, this cat, this villainous film-cartoon cat, running two-footed and two-fisted, treads on the upturned fangs of garden rakes, flattens his features on flapping fence-boards, rolls up like a blind on sudden laundry-lines, is piledriven chin-deep by a toppling telegraph pole, fragmented by falling masonry, paunched by a flying anvil, and still, still pursues, unrelenting and undeterred. How will he catch his quarry? His catty gift of climbing is useless. The canary has grease, to pour down the pole; has a cross-cut saw, for lopping off branches; can whisk out from some recess of its tiny plumage a large black object, bearing the legend *1 cwt*, which it will deposit in the obligingly upturned paws of the horrified feline, just as he is about to complete his ascent of the bird table. Well, then – the rocket deftly strapped to the spine with four expert hitches and a dainty reef-knot on the midriff? Disastrous; the telephone wires deflect its course, and poor pussy explodes starrily, nosedown in the rose bed. So what about that length of rope that should swing us neatly through the window of the bedroom where the wretched bird is preening itself? Good, if only our calculations are right; if wrong, we make a raw, spreadeagled hole in the clapboard side of the neat white North American house. Yet here's a notion – a smart technological trick with the lady's stays, providentially found in the ancient steamer trunk in the loft. A pair of wings are manufactured in a trice; soon the cat is airborne and confidently aerobatic; but ah! – presently the laces break, the wings droop, and our hooligan hero plummets heavily onto the prone form of the snoozing bulldog. All expedients are exhausted, it seems; yet wait one moment; still something remains. Grinning apologetically (one might almost say sheepishly), the cat produces from his fur a crayon, and spirits up a large sheet of card, on which he writes, and exhibits to us, the following message: ANYTHING CAN HAPPEN IN A CARTOON. He then uses the same crayon to draw on the air a flight of steps, up which he nimbly skips to reach the branch where the astonished canary is waiting, for once not wholly prepared.

6.2 AND A LITTLE COMMENTARY

Anyone who has seen film cartoons of the 'Sylvester and Tweety-Pie' or 'Tom and Jerry' variety will recognize the content and conventional absurdities of 'Anything Can Happen'. These animals – or perhaps one should say these *animates* – enact their comic conflict in a world which straddles the frontier of natural law and fabulous licence. At the narrator's convenience the cat runs upright, like a man, or scampers four-footed, like a domestic beast; here he makes a fist and grips tools, there his claws snag in the curtains or the carpet; now, resplendent in straw boater and blazer, he dashes off a note to his ladylove, and then, in furry ignorance, curls up in his basket in front of the fire. The meaning of 'anything can happen' is that the impossible is available in free conjunction with the possible, and furthermore that 'impossible' actions, events, *etc*, have analogies in possibility, analogies just strong enough to give passing credence to what is patently absurd.

The partners to such fantasy – the narrator/presenter and the spectator/reader – are united in their knowledge of its rules and conventions; above all, they know where the 'frontier of natural law' lies, and whenever it is crossed they are perfectly well aware of the fact. They are, indeed, schooled in the conventions of a type of narrative. 'Anything Can Happen' exhibits a further degree of artistic self-awareness, in that one of the *characters* in the story – the cat – is allowed to reflect on, and manipulate, the devices of this kind of fable-making. Despite this sophistication, however, our cartoon tale has the crude limitations of mere fantasy. Anything can happen, but nothing can develop. The cartoon maker is content to go on exploiting one factor of comic narrative, the factor of likelihood.

6.3 THE 'LIKELIHOOD' FACTOR

Many jokes and humorous anecdotes have a 'likelihood' factor, which is to say, they require the acceptance of some absurd proposition or representation. This acceptance may in some cases be taken for granted, simply because it is necessary to the joke, while in others an attempt is made to create grounds of plausibility, by adjusting the conditions we would normally require before accepting a statement, *etc* as 'true'. In illustration of this, let us consider as a philosophical proposition the statement *Sylvester is a man.* This assertion entails other assertions, upon which it is conditional, *ie*:

1. *Sylvester is a human being*
2. *Sylvester is adult*
3. *Sylvester is male*

These entailments express the 'truth conditions' of the statement *Sylvester is a man*, and, indeed, might qualify as a sufficient paraphrase of it: *Sylvester is an adult male human being* is tantamount to *Sylvester is a man*. If however, any one of the entailments fails, then the parent statement is also compromised. *Sylvester is a male human being* is not a *sufficient* paraphrase of *Sylvester is a man*; *Sylvester is an adult male gorilla* is patently a *false* paraphrase.

By the same reasoning, the statement *Sylvester is a tomcat* would entail the following:

1. *Sylvester is a feline animal*
2. *Sylvester is adult*
3. *Sylvester is male*

These resemble the entailments of *Sylvester is a man* closely enough for us to be tempted by the notion of superimposing one set on the other:

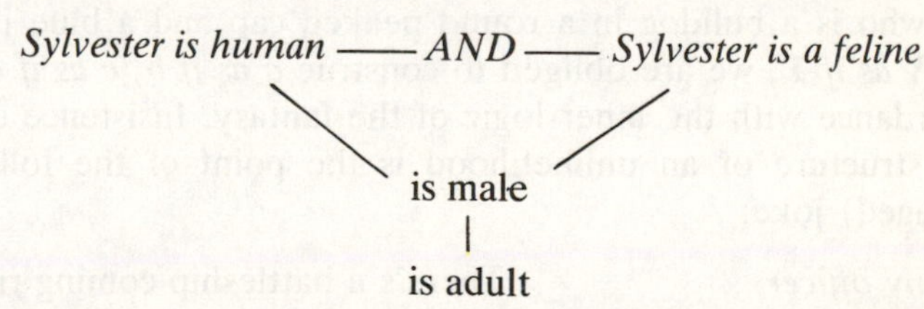

This, of course, is the basis of the likelihood game in the cartoon. The cartoonist studiously explores visual representations of the false paraphrase (*Sylvester is a man* = *Sylvester is a male adult feline*) or the insufficient paraphrase (*Sylvester is a tomcat* = *Sylvester is a male adult*) until felinity either alternates with humanity, or merges with it, or is overlapped by it:

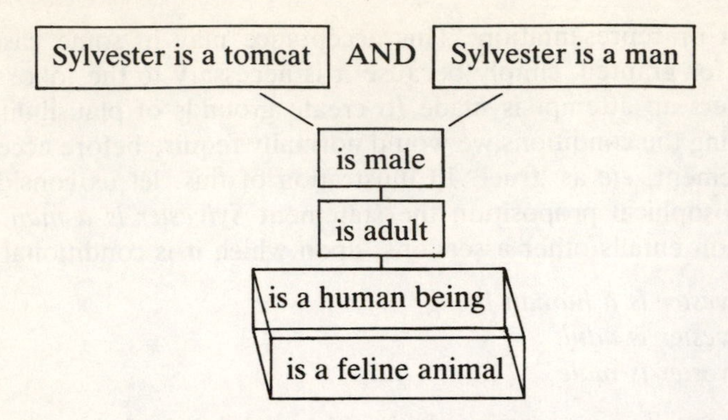

The cartoon requires that an audience should accept the model of feline humanity and/or human felinity. Once that is accepted as plausible there is no difficulty in accepting anything else; and the plausibility is quite readily established because, as we have seen above, it requires the adjustment of only one entailment in a defining set. (The fact that many of us habitually perform this exercise in our relationships with domestic pets no doubt makes the cartoon narrator's task all the easier.)

Only the literal-minded balk at lapses of likelihood in narrative. Although the rest of us also know that cats do not speak, or drink through straws, or wear bow ties, or ride trains, we are glad to accept the condition *as if*, which defines or nullifies the frontier between likely and unlikely. When we allow the narrative to proceed *as if* cats could ride trains, we also allow the consequences of *as if* – *eg* that the cat has lost his ticket and is put off the train by a conductor who is a bulldog in a round peaked cap and a blue jacket. Given *X as if Y*, we are obliged to construe *a as if b*, *c as if d*: *etc*, in accordance with the inner logic of the fantasy. Insistence on the logical structure of an unlikelihood is the point of the following (fairly aged) joke:

Army officer (interviewing candidate for commission):	'There's a battleship coming right at you, across that field. What do you do?'
Candidate (promptly):	'Torpedo it.'

Officer: 'Where d'you get your torpedo?'

Candidate: 'Same place you got your battleship.'

The candidate accepts the officer's opening proposition as an invitation to exploit the likelihood of *as if*. Accordingly, he constructs an answer that respects the proportions of the fantasy: battleship *as if* land vehicle, therefore torpedo *as if* shell, etc. The problem is intelligently treated as a matter of cartoon semantics (so to speak). Reference is less important than the *terms* of reference, a fact which the candidate appears to grasp more confidently than the interviewing officer.

In many flights of humorous fantasy, the point and power of the anecdote lie not so much in the reader/listener's reaction to some gross departure from likelihood, as in the responses of characters within the story. This often characterizes 'shaggy dog' jokes like the following:

> On the first evening after moving into his new house, Bob went down to the local pub, and there fell into conversation with a friendly barman, a man full of local knowledge and a useful source of information on interesting places and strange events. Presently their talk was interrupted by the arrival of a dapper little man, evidently a regular, who greeted the barman, ordered a large glass of sherry, drank it, said goodnight, walked up the wall, across the ceiling, down the opposite wall, and so out through the double door. After this performance there was a short silence before Bob said, quaveringly:
>
> 'Wow! Did you say strange?'
>
> 'Yes,' mused the barman. 'That *was* strange. He usually drinks whisky.'

Clearly the joke here is not about an unlikely event (the gravity-defying walk), but about a *response* to that event, the barman's response. His notions of likelihood and those of Bob are so much at variance that they lead to incompatible readings of a crucial phrase: (page 108).

The barman has excluded the supernatural from his framework of commentary. His perception of likelihood is such that *anything*

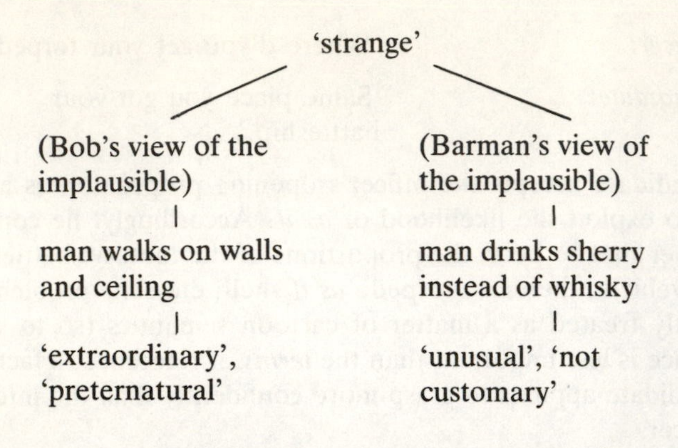

can happen; it is the privileged world of the cartoon. (Note that the entry into 'privileged worlds' is often marked by the frontier-feature – the rabbit-hole, the looking-glass, the stairway, the door.) The fact that anything can happen, however, does not mean that nothing will be perceived as remarkable. It is part of the joke that even in a world of suspended physics people are expected to follow common patterns of minor behaviour; the law of gravity lapses, but the force of habit remains. Therefore, even though anything can happen, the barman can still perceive something out of the ordinary.

From Bob's point of view, the wall-walking episode is more than out of the ordinary; his quavering comment means 'It's impossible', or 'I wouldn't believe it if I hadn't seen it'. For the purposes of the story, he is *committed* to a view of likelihood; his astonishment (contrasted with the low-key reponse of the barman) arises out of that commitment. He *must* believe – his role in the narrative demands it – that this is a preternatural event. In this, the character-within-the-tale possibly differs from the listener/reader, the audience of the story. Our perception of reality is the same as Bob's, but we are not committed to it in the same way; if we were, we would not be so ready to stand back and laugh. We accept that the outrageous thing *does* happen, and by that acceptance we have access to the humour of the barman's response. Unlikelihood does not provoke in us an astonishment from which we cannot free our minds. We accept the impossible as a theoretical postulate, the necessary condition of the joke. With regard to this particular anecdote, three different responses are evident:

Bob's response: *People can't walk on ceilings*
Barman's response: *People can walk on ceilings*
Audience's response: *People can walk on ceilings, even though people can't walk on ceilings*

This can be generalized, *mutatis mutandis*, as a principle of narrative. The audience is persuaded to suspend disbelief, or take a neutral position on matters of likelihood.

6.4 THE 'LOGIC' FACTOR

Every comic unlikelihood operates its own compelling logic; but some logics stand in their own humorous right, as self-contained games with language. An obvious example is the old joke sometimes attributed to Groucho Marx, who is supposed to have asked one of his victims, *Have you stopped beating your wife*? The wicked beauty of the jest is that it catches the respondent off balance, with a false or undesirable presupposition, *ie* number 1 in the following set:

1. Julius beats his wife
2. Julius has stopped beating his wife
3. Julius has not stopped beating his wife

Before either 2 or 3 can be the case, 1 must also be the case. Julius can of course evade the presuppositional trap by saying 'I have never beaten her', or something of the sort. However, the very form of the question helps to draw him into the mechanism of a destructive entailment. It is a form that ordinarily requires a *yes/no* answer (*cf*:*Have you read Tristram Shandy*? or *Have you stopped taking German lessons*?), and in normal interactions it is assumed that *yes* or *no* is a sufficient and unambiguous reply. Groucho's Fork painfully catches anyone who tries to answer *his* question with a yes or a no; the simple affirmative or negative alike concede the outrageous presupposition:

Have you stopped beating your wife?
– *Yes*

(= 'I beat my wife')

Have you stopped beating your wife?
– *No*

(= 'I beat my wife')

This is a language-game, funny in that it mocks the mind entangled in its own symbolic procedures. The game supersedes the reality of what the words convey; wife-beating is an extremely unfunny subject.

Though we may admire their wit, and though philosophers may collect them for tutorial purposes, our response to jokes that turn on logic or the manipulation of language is an uneasy one. They attack our security in a way that is never apparent with jokes based on elaborate breaches of likelihood. It is easy enough to say 'anything can happen', and then stand neutral, like the audience of the Bob-and-the-barman story. What is much less easy is to say 'there is something amiss with this reasoning', and then refrain from a concern to put things right, to restore the intellectual grasp of things, whether for ourselves or for some exponent character in fiction. 'Where's the catch?', we ask, fretfully using a word significantly suggestive of involvement, detention, entrapment. The catch is some kind of philosophical lapse, a false entailment, a defectively formulated proposition, an unjustified predication. It may be the encircling logic for which Joseph Heller has given us a label – *Catch-22*. In the book of that name, the predicament of the desperate American bomber crews is presented in terms that can be summarized as follows:

1. If and only if you are crazy, you can ask to be relieved from combat duty.
2. Anyone who asks to be relieved from combat duty is not crazy.
3. If you ask to be relieved from combat duty you are by definition disqualified from being relieved.

This is the root joke of the book – a grim joke, since all the characters are snagged on Catch-22, and seem to be condemned to its workings until the war kills them. Their fate is to operate within a closed system of argument which envelops all, and from which they cannot escape because they have recourse only to propositions generated within the system. No one can say, 'Being of sound mind, I pronounce myself crazy.' Nor, for purposes of attestation, can he appeal to the squadron medical officer, because the doctor, also involved in the system, is regarded as crazy too: how can a crazy man pronounce on someone else's craziness? The airmen are thus prisoners in the charmlessly charmed military circle. The obvious escape from the catch is for an outsider to come along (this happens in fairy-tales), break the circle, and set the captives free. An independent, 'extra-circular' doctor would do wonders for the hapless airmen of Catch-22; but there is no such person in Heller's narrative. The crews have no rescuing angel, no redeemer from elsewhere; though at the end of the book one of the pilots brings hope by escaping to neutral Sweden, breaking out of the manic war-prison, leaping over its murderous logic. That social and institutional systems trap their members in the pinch of absurd but apparently inescapable arguments is the besetting nightmare of the book, and also the source of its undoubted humour. The lunatic precision of the argument itself makes us laugh, through episodes in which the underlying reality is tragic or pathetic. Catch-22 logic invades the most trivial situations. There is, for example, a rumbustious episode in which Yossarian, the hero, sentimentally asks an Italian streetwalker to marry him. She tells him that he is crazy to want to marry her, because she is not a virgin. When he replies that he will marry her nonetheless, she protests that she cannot marry anyone who is crazy. When he asks her why he is crazy, she says it is because he wants to marry her. This is the kind of reasoning that R. D. Laing has frequently observed in psychiatric patients, and has recorded in the verbal patterns of the book called *Knots*. The following extract, entitled *Jill*, is strong on Catch-22 logic:

I don't respect myself
I can't respect anyone who respects me
I can only respect someone who does not respect me.

I respect Jack
because he does not respect me

I despise Tom
because he does not despise me

Only a despicable person
can respect someone as despicable as me

I cannot love someone I despise

Since I love Jack
I cannot believe he loves me

What proof can he give? [18]

This woman is the victim of her personal closed system, just as the airmen of Catch-22 are victimized by an institutional closed system. For such prisoners, what is the alternative to despair? Looking on, we say 'You have to laugh, or it would drive you crazy.'

Writers whose humour relies extensively on the manipulations of logic are often adept at creating closed systems from which a hero-victim can escape only by some process of magic, some accident, or some act of will. These systems are based on a few common types of logical malpractice, *eg* the false syllogism, the mismanagement of *because* and *therefore*, confusions in the scope of *all*, *some*, *many*, *most*: *etc*, the attribution of positive reference to a negative sign. It is the kind of humour at which Lewis Carroll excels, and which has made him the darling of philosophers seeking to put laughter in its rational place. Carroll's games with negation are well known:

> 'What do you know about this business?' the King said to Alice.
>
> 'Nothing,' said Alice.
>
> 'Nothing *whatever*?' persisted the King.
>
> 'Nothing whatever,' said Alice.
>
> 'That's very important,' the King said, turning to the jury. They were just beginning to write this down on their slates, when the White Rabbit interrupted: '*Un*important, your Majesty means of course,' he said, in a very respectful tone, but frowning and making faces at him as he spoke.
>
> '*Un*important, of course, I meant,' the King hastily said, and went on to himself in an undertone, 'important – unimportant – unimportant – important – ' as if he were trying which word sounded best.
>
> Some of the jury wrote it down 'important', and some 'unimportant'. Alice could see this, as she was near enough to look over their slates; 'but it doesn't matter a bit,' she thought to herself. [5; p 155]

Alice is not wholly right; it *does* matter a bit. The officiousness of the White Rabbit has confounded the King's formally correct (if inane) courtroom procedure. When the King says *that's very important* he refers to *the fact that Alice says she knows nothing*; the White Rabbit, however, allows *important* a much narrower scope, as descriptive only of the word *nothing*. He assumes that the King means to say *Nothing is important*. This brings us at one step into the corny country of Carrollian confusion, for *Nothing is important* might imply *Everything is unimportant*, or it could mean, as the White Rabbit apparently suggests, that *A non-existent thing cannot be important*. Hence his insistence that *Nothing is unimportant*, and hence the poor King's experimental mutterings, and the bewilderment of the jurors; for *Nothing is unimportant* can mean that *Everything is important*. So what are the jurors to conclude? That *Nothing is important = Everything is unimportant*, or that *Nothing is unimportant = Everything is important*? It matters more than Alice supposes, although she is right in her intuition that in the world of Wonderland experience it all comes in the end to the same unavailing thing.

The King of Hearts and all his subjects are trapped in a domain of circling logics, where all roads of discourse diverge only to meet again at the same meaningless point. The very location of Carroll's fantasy worlds – at the almost Antipodean end of the rabbit-hole, on the other side of the looking glass – suggests and promotes the humour of inversion and circularity, of the topsy-turvy proposition and the companion image. Alice, as observer, is not completely involved in the closed system. Carroll allows her two protective conditions. One is that she is never taken in. She always perceives something amiss with Wonderglass reasoning, even when she cannot rebut its propositions. The other is that she can escape from the system by a vehemently human reaction – kicking down the cards, trying to throttle the Red Queen – which causes her to wake up. Her cry, *You're nothing but a pack of cards*! is the triumphant, self-liberating declaration of a human being discovering that she need not be dominated by the institutionalized tyranny of mere symbols. Without such provisions, the humour of circular logic becomes the panic of nightmare; only if there is an independent stance or an escape route can we afford to laugh. This may help to explain why some people detest logic-twisting jokes. A distorted logic is feared as a quasi-criminal act, a threat to the regency of the mind.

6.5 THE 'PRAGMATIC' FACTOR

Together with the shifted likelihood and the dislocated logic goes a third major source of humour: the waywardness of words missing their mark in ordinary conversational interactions. The philosopher J. L. Austin has reminded us that words not only *mean* something, as signs referring to objects, concepts, *etc*, but also *do* something. In daily life they operate as *acts*, so that when, for example, I pay the milkman, handing over the money and at the same time saying *Three pounds sixty-five*, my words have significance not as the statement of a calculation, but as the marker of a transaction. The milkman understands this, and as a rule will acknowledge the act with some conventional expression of confirmation. His *That's right*, or *Quite correct*, does not mean that he has counted the money, but that he has noted my act of payment and is performing his own act of reception. However, if he should one day reply *And I bet you wish it wasn't*, he will have made a mild joke by ignoring or 'by-passing' the pragmatic significance of my words and drawing attention to their referential meaning.

Humour of this kind is very common. Here, for example, are two jokes with many magazine variants:

1. *Clergyman*: 'I now pwonounce you man and wife.'
   Bride: 'And you pwonounce it beautifully, Wector.'
2. *Clerk of the Court*: 'How do you find the defendant? Guilty or not guilty?'
   Foreman of the Jury: 'Guilty isn't the word.'

Joke 1 is doubly pointed. The first point is that the bride has the same speech defect as the clergyman. We might thus regard it simply as a joke about mispronunciation. There is a second and more important point, however. The clergyman's words – a formula from the marriage service – are a performative speech act, signifying that at this moment, by virtue of his office, the man and woman before him become a married couple. *Pronounce* does not mean 'the way I say these words', but rather, 'what I do with these words'. The bride, however, chooses to interpret *pronounce* in the former sense.

Joke 2 invites similar commentary. It exploits the meaning of *find* ((i) make a verdict, (ii) form an impression of), so that this word becomes a *locus*, without which the exchange must lose some of its comic point. Yet this does not wholly explain the joke, which must be interpreted as a defective or misfiring speech-act. The clerk's query is not a query but a charge (= 'tell the court'), and it has a rigidly predicated response (= 'say either *guilty* or *not guilty*') This is the act of pronouncing (*pronounce again!*) a verdict. Replies such as *Very, very guilty, Kinda guilty, I guess. Pretty guilty, all things considered*, *Guiltyish*: *etc* are not appropriate to this verdictive act.

The foreman in the joke behaves as though he were asked to evaluate the state of guilt (how guilty is guilty?) and not merely to indicate a decision. In Crown Courts in Britain it is currently the practice for the Clerk of the Court to say to the foreman of the Jury, *Answer this question yes or no: have you arrived at a verdict*? The reason for the strict injunction to *answer yes or no* is plain; what is required is a simple speech act, the rendering of a verbal token to mark a point in the institutional proceedings. Were the instruction omitted, and were the foreman bold enough to abort the speech act, some funny exchanges might result:

Clerk: 'Have you arrived at a verdict?'
Foreman: 'Arrived! My dear, *I'm* still travelling.'
or
'I don't know if we've arrived, but we've managed to get somewhere.'
or
'Well, yes, it was pretty hard going until teatime, with seven against five, but after a pot of tea and those lovely macaroons, three came over, making it ten against two, so that's a majority, is that OK?'

Fortunately or unfortunately, the rituals of the court preclude such outbursts.

Here, in this perverse strain of humour, we encounter one of the most important functions of language, as an expression of social cohesion in the various interactions of everyday life. To disturb this function is either to draw attention to some oddity in the way the interaction is habitually formulated, or, more seriously, to imply an act of rejection, whether of institutions, customs, or persons. The first of these possibilities is attested in many a junior joke-book:

Diner: 'Waiter, what's this fly doing in my soup?'
Waiter: 'Looks like the breast-stroke, sir.'

The diner's question is to be understood, in its social function, as an act of complaint; he is not asking for information, though the waiter chooses to interpret his words in that sense. The joke sports with a peculiarity of English social usage, which resorts to the meaningfully oblique question in the expression of directives, reservations, or complaints. Thus, *Aren't those my bags*? may be tantamount to *Go and fetch them; May I think about it*? probably means *I'm going to reject this proposal*; and *Isn't this cloth a bit grubby*? signifies *I strongly object to filthy table linen*.

Such oblique questions do not always deserve, or get, friendly answers. The waiter in the following exchange refuses to play the social game, and his refusal has implications that go beyond pleasant commentary on the oddities of social language:

> *Diner*: 'Isn't this cloth a bit off colour?'
> *Waiter*: 'Wait till you see your lobster.'

Is the waiter joking? Or is he frustrating the intended directive (= 'Change the tablecloth') in order to mark his rebuttal of an implied rebuke? ('Don't try that game with me'; 'I won't be patronized by sardonic remarks'). Or, a further possibility, does his retort signify a denial of the importance of clean tablecloths? ('What's all the fuss about? You came here to *eat*, didn't you?') The doubt, and the lurking possibility of ironic contrivance, occur because such exchanges violate the maxims of 'ordinary' conversation, as formulated in a well-known paper by H. P. Grice. [45] Grice discusses at length the tacit acceptance, by participants in conversation, of the obligation to give adequate and accurate information, not to be prolix, not to get into conversational deadlocks, not to be snagged on *non-sequiturs*, to pay attention to what is said, to try to make relevant assertions and responses. These obligations are summarized in four broad maxims, of *Quantity* (*eg* supply sufficient, and appropriate, information), of *Quality* (*eg* do not become involved in an evidently pointless conversation), of *Relation* (*eg* be relevant) and of *Manner* (*eg* be concise and avoid obscurity). The work of Grice, of Austin, and of J. R. Searle, puts into theoretical terms what we already know intuitively about conversation, *ie* that it is a contract involving the agreed conduct of various acts of assertion, direction, performance, verdict-giving, promising, inviting, requesting, *etc*. When the contract is broken, whether innocently or designedly, the effect may be funny; may illuminate a character or situation; or may designate some critical defect in a relationship. Not surprisingly, the humour of psychological and social satire is expressed to a very great extent through the flaws and missed connections of speech acts, the contractual failures of parties to conversation.

6.6 FOUR PARADIGMS OF DEFECTIVE EXCHANGE

We may illustrate the 'contractual failure' by citing four common and easily recognizable types of conversational hang-up. The typological nicknames are for purposes of convenient reference:

Hang-up no. 1: the 'runaround'

Example:

A: 'And where do you work, Mr Jones?'
B: 'Oh, you know, at the Town Hall.'
A: 'And what do you do there?'
B: 'Oh, you know, Town Hall work.'

Comment:Grice's maxim of Quantity (calling for sufficient and appropriate information) is flouted, and with it the maxim of Quality that warns against pointless conversations. Whether by design or in mere stupidity, *A* is given the runaround; this conversation gets him nowhere.

Hang-up no 2: the 'skid'

Example:

A: 'Now you take the whale, that's just about the oldest fish in the ocean.'
B: 'It isn't a fish. It's a mammal. The whale is a mammal.'
A: 'Well, the Bible says it's a fish. The oldest book in the world says the whale is a fish.'
B: 'Look, they just didn't know enough in those days. They had a naive taxonomy. If it swam in the sea, they classified it as a fish. We know better now, we know the whale is a mammal.'
A: 'You're telling me the author of the Bible didn't know what he was doing? The Bible? The book you swear on in court?'

Comment: *A* produces – knowingly or unknowingly – a piece of misinformation, which *B* decides – prudently or imprudently – to correct. The conversation then goes into a skid, which becomes worse as *B* tries to correct it. All the Gricean rules are side-swiped. Most skids begin in simple ignorance, but it is possible to start them deliberately, with mischievously designed propositions: 'The duodenum, along with the other so-called organs of speech, has two functions'; 'Julius Caesar, as is well known, was never completely converted to Christianity'; 'Lightning, striking *upwards*, produces the optical illusion of striking *downwards*.'

Hang-up no. 3: the 'backhander'

Example:

A: 'Let's go for a picnic.'
B: 'A picnic! In this weather! You must be out of your mind.'
A: 'All right, let's stay home and listen to some records.'
B: 'That's just like you – no drive, no imagination.'

Comment: This is the familiar conversational behaviour of the nagging or implacable partner, who counters all suggestions cussedly, with a series of rebuffs, or 'backhanders'. The maxim of Quality is breached; it is quite pointless for *A* to push on with this conversation, though he/she may well do so in an attempt to make a domestic concord with *B*.

Hang-up no. 4: the 'googly' (or 'spitball')

Example:

A: 'How would you like to spend seven days in a Portuguese villa?'
B: 'I'd *love* it!'
A: 'Good, then you can envy me all next week.'

Comment: The player – in this case, *B* – is deceived by the teasing flight and spin of the ball. He not unreasonably anticipates an invitation; and he is cruelly caught out. Inasmuch as *A*'s question is intentionally misleading, it may be said to offend doubly, against the maxims of Quantity (give enough information) and Manner (avoid obscurity). *A* might have pitched up a straightforward delivery – 'I'm going to spend next week in a Portuguese villa. Don't you envy me?'; but he prefers to bowl a googly. It isn't cricket.

6.7 THE DEFECTIVE EXCHANGE AS A CHARACTERIZING MOTIF IN COMIC FICTION

Some works of fiction exploit the defective exchange, not simply as an occasional device of humour, but as an element in the very fabric of the work, expressing character, typifying relationships, and framing situations. Such a work is Joseph Heller's *Good as Gold*, the theme of which has been outlined elsewhere (see §4.6). Bruce Gold's relationships with family, friends and acquaintances are all defective relationships, and tend to be characterized by defective conversational exchanges. It is one of Gold's ambitions to become a White House official and to penetrate the secrets of the American political establishment. To do so, however, he must come to semantic terms with his friend Ralph Newsome, and Ralph's discourse is frankly impenetrable:

> 'You'll like it here, won't you?' said Ralph, reading his mind.
> 'Is it always like this?'
> 'Oh, yes,' Ralph assured him. 'It's always like this when it's this way.'
> Gold succeeded in speaking without sarcasm. 'How is it when it isn't?'
> Isn't what, Bruce?'
> 'This way.'
> 'Different.'
> 'In what way, Ralph?'
> 'In different ways, Bruce, unless they're the same, in which case it's this way.'
> 'Ralph,' Gold had to ask, 'don't people here laugh or smile when you talk that way?'
> 'What way, Bruce?'
> 'You seem to qualify or contradict all your statements.'
> 'Do I?' Ralph considered the matter intently. 'Maybe I do seem a bit oxymoronic at times. I think everyone here talks that way. Maybe we're all oxymoronic.' [16; p 128]

Ralph has natural skill in the runaround. He describes his White House function as 'unnamed government spokesman', and likes it because he gets into the papers pretty often. In passage after passage – in fact, whenever he appears in the book – he destroys meaningful conversation through contradictory or self-cancelling propositions, irrelevant responses, and redundant or 'circular'information. ('What is your area?' Gold asks him at one point. 'Just about everything I cover,' says Ralph, and when Gold persists, with 'What do you cover?' replies 'Everything in my area.') The effect of all this obsessive play with the unresponsive response is to create for the reader the comic character of Ralph Newsome, Government Spokesman, and to do so much more effectively than pages of description and analysis. Ralph's character is nothing that can be effectively described *by* words. It resides *in* words; his soul is a self-adjusting verbal framework which is never allowed to pull out of balance, much less to tremble under the weight of anything like a meaning. The character of Ralph, however, also symbolizes the administration and the political culture Gold so desperately wants to enter but cannot for one moment penetrate. As far as the White House is concerned, the runaround rules, OK.

In his relationships with his family, Gold is plagued by the circumstance of being the clever youngest child, the college professor and writer, who is admired but who has to be taken down a peg, whenever the family congregates, for his own good. His brother Sid, a harder case than Humpty Dumpty, specializes in the controlled skid, sending Gold whirling with outrageous propositions such as 'Pyrenees is the only language in the world which has no words for right or left.' Occasionally Sid is aided and abetted by other members of the family who enjoy teasing Bruce:

> Esther . . . asked, 'Sometimes when I look out my window in winter, I see ice flowing up the river – why is that?'
>
> 'That's because ice is lighter than water,' answered Sid, 'and it's floating up to get to the top of the river.'
>
> For an instant Gold was speechless. Blood rushed to his face. 'Do you really think,' he demanded in a cold fury, 'that the ice is flowing up to get to the top of the river?'
>
> 'Isn't it?' asked Sid.
>
> 'Do you really think that up is up?' Gold blurted out, pointing northward angrily.
>
> 'Up isn't up,' said someone.
>
> 'Sure, it's up,' said someone else.
>
> 'What then, it's down?' answered still one more.
>
> 'I meant north,' Gold corrected himself with a shout. 'Do you really think that something is higher just because it's north?'
>
> Sid preserved a tranquil silence while others championed his cause. [16; p 111]

This is affectionate baiting, only faintly tinged with malice, but it makes Gold hate family occasions, when he feels 'lonely as an oyster'.

Gold's father, an immigrant Jew in an alien culture, vindictive, self-pitying, hating the *goyim*, struggles furiously to assert his authority over his dutiful children, some of whom are cleverer and more successful than he. In his dealings with his youngest child, he is grimly intractable, an opponent of every assertion, unwilling to concede the most trivial point, refusing to agree with the most harmless opinion. Here Gold suggests an outing to a restaurant:

> 'Let's go to Lundy's,' he suggested. 'It's right here. We'll have a good piece of fish.'
> 'What's so good about it?' said his father.
> 'So' – Gold declined to argue – 'it won't be so good.'
> 'Why you getting me fish that's no good?' [16; *p* 98]

The elder Gold's conversational speciality is the backhander. His *What's so good about it*? is not an interested query; it is plainly contentious, and means something like 'I don't believe the fish will be any good.' Bruce's *So it won't be so good* is an utterance falling into the same category as *Maybe so*, *Perhaps not*, *You could be right*, *Anything you say* – remarks that note and acknowledge, *non-committally*, the expression of an opinion. His father, however, deliberately and perversely misinterprets the acknowledging sign as *committal* to the opinion expressed: *So it won't be so good* = 'I agree that it will not be good.' Hence he delivers his second backhander, *Why you getting me fish that's no good*? There is a concomitant perversion of usage in his adroit conversion of *not so good* (= 'only fair', 'not especially good', 'no better than anyone else's') into *no good* (= 'bad'). This simply cantankerous nature expresses itself in a cussed and complicated semantics.

There is another appalling old man in the book, the polar counterpart, as savage gentile, of Gold's father, the savage Jew. This is Pugh Biddle Conover, rich, influential, virulently anti-Semitic, a wheelchair invalid, father of the glamorous and nubile girl whose favours Gold laboriously enjoys and whom he intends to marry (at Ralph Newsome's insistence) after he has disposed of his less glamorous Jewish wife. When Gold is invited to spend a weekend at the Conovers', his host greets him on the first morning with malign good humour:

'Ah, good morning, dear fellow,' he greeted him warmly. 'Did you sleep well?'

'Indeed I did,' Gold responded with eagerness to the unexpected clubby sociability of his host. 'The room was a castle and the bed was superb.'

'I'm sorry to hear that,' said Conover cheerfully. 'Enjoy your breakfast?'

'Immensely'

'Too bad,' said Conover, and Gold welled with sorrow again. [16; *p* 255]

Conover has various conversational stratagems for confusing and humiliating Gold. One of them is the googly, as illustrated here. A ritual of sociability is predicted by Conover's opening remark:

'Did you sleep well?'

'Indeed I did.'

'I'm pleased to hear that. Enjoy your breakfast?'

'Immensely.'

'That's good.'

This is an act of phatic communion, an exchange of speech-tokens importing the friendship and social solidarity of the speakers – a kind of verbal handshaking or nose-rubbing. Gold has every right to expect a conventional enactment of the ritual, and is prepared to supply the appropriate responses. He is deceived, however, and plays into his enemy's twisting hands. His 'correct' expressions of satisfaction and pleasure, as guest to host, leave him open to insult, and enable Conover to play the dual role of host and enemy. Conover's demeanour is 'correct' and host-like in accordance with the ritual; he behaves 'warmly' and 'cheerfully'. His words, on the other hand, are inimical. This short exchange exemplifies his twisted nature, the warping of his personality in mind and body.

The people with whom Gold associates in one relationship or another all have a knack of significantly breaking the conversational rules, leaving the highly articulate Gold (who can also break a rule when he needs to) at various kinds of disadvantage. He is in Alice's position – with Sid for Humpty Dumpty and Ralph for Mad Hatter – but he is not allowed Alice's saving detachment, or her power to evade the dangerously enveloping fantasy by some self-willed act of disruption. His redemption, if that is the right word, comes when

Sid throws his final skid, in the form of a fatal heart attack which strikes him just as Gold is preparing to meet the President at an Embassy Ball. 'He does this to me every time', says Gold; but it is Sid's death that leads him to reconsider his relationships, his Jewishness, and his absurd hankering for a White House career.

To claim that the whole content and texture of a complex novel like *Good as Gold* might be expounded in terms of typical conversational patterns is patently absurd. Comedy is always deeper than the verbal game, and all the explanation of jokes and ironies and topsy-turvy argument cannot come to terms with the manifold truths of character and situation. Furthermore, there is a parodic richness in the text that may only be fully enjoyed by a reader who is both American and Jewish. Nevertheless, exchanges of the type examined above are consistently related to the *infrastructure* of the novel, just as, in other instances, anecdotes may have infrastructural significance. (On 'infrastructure', see §3.4.) The reader who fails to see how these segments of jesting dialogue are part of a general commentary on a world of misapprehensions may taste their humour, but will miss their comedy.

Seven

Language in its humour: (i) manipulations of meaning

7.1 'LAYERING'

We may ask – the question has haunted several chapters – whether 'the language of comedy', 'the language of humour', and 'humorous language' are equivalent expressions? Do comic style and structure necessarily imply a profusion of jokes and witticisms? To pose the question in this way is perhaps to answer it. We imply that 'the language of comedy' may be quite unremarkable, sentence for sentence – may, indeed, be deliberately banal – but that 'the language of humour', and certainly 'humorous language' must always be characterized by a tension attributable to devices latent in the linguistic system, possibilities realized by *language in its humour*. What possibilities, then? And how are they realized?

First, as we have noted elsewhere, jesting language is frequently 'layered', working its effects combinatively through sounds, through vocabulary, and through grammar and syntax. In this convergence of linguistic elements, it resembles – obviously – the language of poetry. As an example, let us consider possible transformations of a sentence not in itself strikingly humorous:

1. My watch fell into the river.

From this emerges, with a little playful tinkering:

2. My timepiece toppled into the Thames.

And again:

3. Into the Thames toppled my timepiece.

Although it is begging the question to assert that 2 and 3 are humorous, readers will at least recognize a facetious intent, manifested through peculiar intensities of linguistic patterning. We note, for instance, the alliteration of '*t*imepiece', '*t*opple', and '*Th*ames', a joking impulse in the management of *sound*. This, however, is obviously not the whole joke. The sounds are linked with significant lexical items, *timepiece* and *topple*, which strike the native observer as in some way out of the ordinary. *Timepiece*, he thinks, is a funny way of saying 'watch', and *topple* is a whimsical expression of 'fall' There is an oddity, he might add, in the juxtaposition, or *collocation*, of these two words as exponents of 'actor' and 'action'. Trees topple; dynamited chimneys topple; slain giants topple; governments topple; even theories topple; but not timepieces of the wrist- or pocket-watch variety. Evidently there is something distinctive about the re-casting in 2 and 3, not only in terms of *sound*, but also in the *lexicon*. Version 3 presents a further point of distinction. Here the syntax of the basic sentence is changed, so that the adjunct *into the Thames* is moved into a position at the beginning of the clause, while the subject *My timepiece* goes to the end of the sentence, after the verb. This inversion has an effect of rhetorical heightening and suspense, the kind of effect a raconteur might seek in shaping the performance of a joke. In version 3, then, the element of a distinctive *syntax* is incorporated with a distinctive *lexicon* and a distinctive pattern of *sound*. This humorous language is thus *layered*.

The original sentence, *My watch fell into the river*, shows none of these extraordinary contrivances. There is no apparent *locus* of humour, no brilliance or peculiar density of patterning; nothing alliterates, rhymes, or chimes, the lexical items are quite ordinary, the syntactic structure of Subject-Verb-Adjunct has nothing remarkable about it. In isolation the sentence is not in the least humorous – which does not mean that it has no comic potential. It might very easily claim a place at the focal point of a comic narration:

> The dandy strolls by the river– hears a cry for help – sees the floundering bather – is torn between the laws of humanity and the levies of vanity – oh! my handmade shirt! my Jaeger socks! – hesitates – decides at least to remove his 24-carat solid gold multijewelled Swiss action thirty day wrist-watch before taking the merciful plunge – lays it down on the bank near his straw hat and Irish linen handkerchief – leaps into the water – is greatly encumbered by his doeskin blazer and Italian leather shoes – kicks off the footwear – sloughs the haberdashery – is half-way to his objective when the police launch arrives and rescues the distressed swimmer – gives a wave and a comradely shout – is curtly informed that bathing is prohibited – begins to swim back – clothing still an impediment – is obliged to divest himself of his good grey

cavalry twill trousers – reaches bank at last – quite exhausted – hauls himself up, hand over hand – reaches the top with one last wild sweep of the arm – hand strikes something solid, and –

My watch fell into the river.

This burlesque outline suggests how a sentence unremarkable in itself might function significantly as an element in the language of comedy. Various possibilities of comic significance suggest themselves. One is the typographical isolation of the sentence, as above, emphasizing its status as a sort of comment or formulate (see §4.6) Another is the overall stylistic strategy of dandifying the language of the narrative (as suggested in some of the sketch-phrases, *eg*: *slough the haberdashery*), until the final sentence, which is deliberately 'flat'. A related procedure would assign to as many sentences as possible the first-person subject – the *I* of the narrator who picks and chooses and controls; the non-personal subject of the final sentence then points up the last humiliating turnabout, the loss of control. (*I came – I saw – I blundered – My watch fell into the river.*) These suggestions do indeed imply a distinction between 'the language of comedy' and 'humorous language'. The larger term concerns a discursive relationship between all the parts of a text and its infrastructure; the narrower concept denotes the stylistic properties of particular utterances (sentences, phrases, words). Needless to say, these notions are not mutually exclusive; there is nothing to prevent an utterance from being both 'humorous' and *comedic*.

7.2 THE 'EXTRINSIC' DEFINITION OF HUMOROUS LANGUAGE

Passing fancy suggests that some items are intrinsically humorous: some sounds, for example, in certain clusters or sequences (*clank*, *squelch*); some words of rare occurrence or extraordinary form (*skulduggery*, *ramshackle*, *shenanigans*, *malfeasance*, *disgruntlement*); even some small items of grandfatherly grammar (*eg*: *notwithstanding* and *whomsoever* and *be it known*). The search for the intrinsically funny, however, like the search for the intrinsically poetic, is a forlorn enterprise. The most likely conjecture about any examples we might suggest is that they have no humorous power in their own right, but are *residually* humorous, *ie* they take a colouring from repeated use in jokes and comic narrative. There are clichés of comic expression, just as there are clichés of poetic expression. The onomatopoeic effect of *clank* (in that whimsical story about our dear old family car); the bizarre and bony emphasis of *skulduggery* (in that tall tale of what went on at the departmental Christmas party); the pedantic bravura of *whomsoever* (in that hilarious account of the donnish desk sergeant down at the local police station) all are comic clichés, patches from the humorist's indispensable rag-bag. They do not become intrinsically humorous through being constantly used for humorous purposes.

In connection with this, it may be supposed that writers help to form the accepted cast of humorous expression, for example by habitually reserving for a comic function one item in a set of synonyms; thus, out of a fairly large selection of words available for the expression of the meaning 'unhappy' – 'depressed', 'dispirited', 'downcast', 'downhearted', *etc* – one might repeatedly choose *glum* as the clown word, the item that has to bear its comic cross. Introspection tells us that such choices are continually made, and it is arguable that they become generalized, as part of a *humorous habit* in English usage. This, however, is a long way from saying that *glum* (or any other such item) bears the imprint of an intrinsic humour.

We are on safer ground if we assume that the properties of humorous expression are defined *extrinsically*, *ie* that words and phrases seem funny because of their contextual linkages and semantic relationships. Some of the defining features are *syntagmatic*, appearing in the repetitions, parallels, inversions, etc, marked out in the linear progression of the text:

(This might express a pattern of alliteration, or a phrase-design of adjectives and nouns)

Others can be described as *paradigmatic*, being selections from a 'zone of choice' or implied set of possibilities, *eg* a group of synonyms:

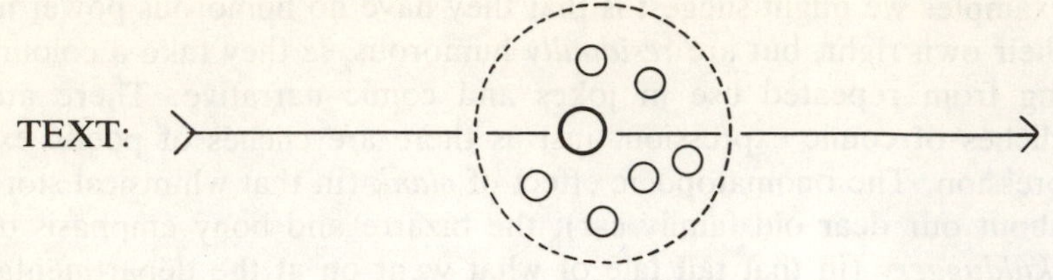

(This would characterize the selection of *glum* out of the set that includes 'dejected', 'depressed', *etc*)

Often the humorous characteristics of a phrase or sentence are both syntagmatic and paradigmatic; the defining features occur both in the *line* and *zone* of the text:

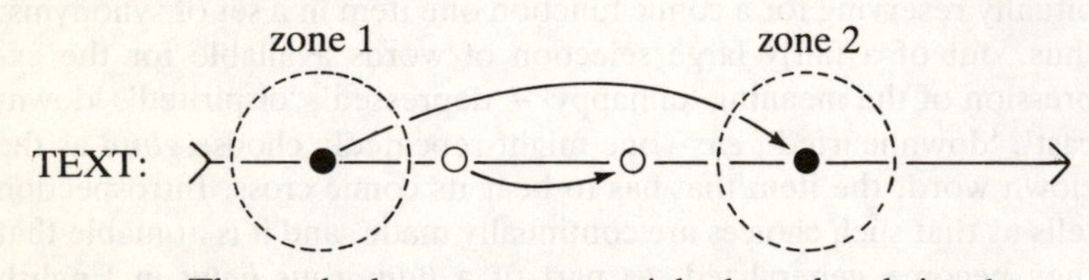

(There is an alliterative sequence, in the textual *line*, combined with significant paradigmatic choices in the *zone* of 'lank' / 'lean', 'thin', 'skinny', 'emaciated' / and 'lugubriously' / 'dolefully', 'sadly', 'mournfully' /)

This last example teaches a lesson. So often, when we are pleased by a humorous text, we attribute a peculiar power to its vocabulary – '*Lank*! What a funny word to use! Why, it even *sounds* funny!' – *etc*. But examination will always show that these apparently dynamic items are not self-charged. They are always located in a context, or *allocated* to a position in a design. (The joking *locus* has its relationship to the *line* and the *zone*.) *Lank*, for instance, is not intrinsically humorous, but is *extrinsically defined* as a potentially humorous point in the context *The lank sergeant sighed lugubriously*. Of such points in such contexts, we may note how they support and, so to speak, safeguard each other. If we do not smile at *lank* we may be cajoled by *lugubriously*; then, if *lugubriously* charms us, we may be retrospectively amused by *lank*.

7.3 SEQUENCES AND SETS

Into the design of his text the humorist incorporates various kinds of rhetorical sequence: sequences of syntactic constructions with their variations, parallels and antitheses, sequences of ideas or 'notions' – 'zonal sequences', as it were – with points of reference and interrelationship located in important words. These syntactic and semantic sequences are sometimes phonetically defined, *eg* in patterns of alliteration:

(a) *continuous:*	'*t*wo *t*erribly *t*ired *t*oads'	*t-t-t-t*
(b) *alternating*:	'*t*orpid *t*oads and *f*ailing *f*rogs'	*t-t / f-f*
(c) *transverse*:	'*f*at *t*oads and *f*risky *t*errapins'	*f-t-f-t*
(d) *inverse*:	'*f*ierce *t*oad, *t*imid *f*rog'	*f-t-t-f*

Such alliterative series give contour to syntactic and semantic groupings, suggesting variations of focus. Example (c) above suggests, through the alliteration, a semantic complement of notions expressed in 'fat' and 'frisky'. Here the alliterative sequence corresponds with the syntactic sequence (adjective+noun, adjective+noun) and the semantic sequence (quality *A* versus complementary/contrasting quality *B*). In example (d) this matching is avoided; the alliterative series cuts across other sequential elements.

Sequencing, as we have already implied, is commonly related to another kind of manipulation, that of choosing from semantic sets. A little playful experiment illustrates this process, taking for our starting point:

Mr Brown's bull mastiff bayed at the bread man

Here is an obvious and simple sequencing device, in the form of continuous alliteration; the verb, however, suggests a 'zone of choice', with the selection of a distinctive item, *bayed*, adding to the humorous colouring of the sentence. Why *bayed*? we may ask. It is not the 'ordinary', or 'usual', or 'core', or 'most general' word. The 'ordinary' and most comprehensive term is *bark*:

BARK	=	the 'ordinary', or 'core', or 'general' word	(= 'superordinate', or 'hyperonym')
yap *snap* *yelp* *bay*	=	the 'particular', or 'special' word	(= 'subordinate', or 'hyponym')

Bark, this scheme suggests, is the most general word, a neutral word, a fairly colourless word. *Yap*, *snap*, *yelp* and *bay* are different types of barking. To say wherein the differences lie, we would have to specify the components of each, in accordance with some regular scheme of description; for instance, we might choose as distinctive criteria 'volume', 'pitch', 'timbre' and 'continuity'. *Bay* suggests 'loud', 'low-pitched', 'resonant' and 'prolonged'; an impressive style of barking that might well intimidate the bread man. But baying is not inappropriate to bull mastiffs. It is, as it were, in the semantic scheme of things:

	'bull mastiff'	collocates with	'bay'
via correspondent semantic features of	size	⟷	loudness
	strength	⟷	resonance, continuity

The case would be decidedly altered if Mr Brown had a poodle, or a chihuahua, or a Mexican hairless, or any dog whose bark is feeble, high-pitched, strident and discontinuous (*ie* any yappy little brute). Then it would be semantically discordant, but humorous, to speak of 'baying' (*Down*, *Alphonse*! *And Fifi, do stop baying at the vicar*!)

Now in extension of our playful experiment we may add to our primary example a further sentence:

> Mr Brown's bull mastiff bayed at the bread man,
> Mrs Thompson's terrier taunted a passing tramp.

This new example is marked, like the original, by an alliterative sequence, and in syntax bears a partial correspondence to its counterpart. (Subject is matched with subject and verb with verb, but the final syntactic element in the first sentence is an adverbial adjunct, whereas in the second it is a direct object.) A striking innovation in the semantics of this second sentence is that the verb, *taunt*, which commonly takes as subject a word denoting a human agent, is here governed by a non-human subject. *Taunt*, we further note, is chosen out of a set that might include 'goad', 'mock', 'deride', 'tease', 'scoff (at)', 'jeer (at)' – words implying, variously, the semantic properties of 'ridicule', 'contempt', 'reproach', 'mimicry', 'provocation', 'dismissiveness'. The significant properties of *taunt* appear to be 'contempt', 'ridicule', 'reproach or upbraiding', plus, of course 'hostility'. *Yah*! says the terrier to the tramp, *I despise you, you sack of rubbish. How can you go around looking like that*? *Clear off before I bite you*. We imagine the terrier speaking, for of course *taunt* implies speech.

At this point, a reconsideration of the original example suggests that we might strengthen the parallel between our two sequences by changing the original verb, *bayed*. There are two requirements. One is, that the substituted verb must begin with *b*, to keep the alliterative pattern unbroken; the other is, that it must be selected from a 'zone of choice' congruent with that of *taunt* – that is, it must be a verb in some way suggestive of mocking speech. These combined demands may force an unusual choice, but the unusual is by no means the enemy of the humorous:

Mr Brown's bull mastiff barracked the bread man.

Barracking is an activity more appropriate to cricket spectators than bull mastiffs, but the word will do nicely; to *barrack* is a legitimate member, if a somewhat exotic one, of the set that includes 'mock', 'taunt', 'jeer', 'scoff', 'deride', 'upbraid'. And now the two example sentences incorporate sequences which are in parallel phonetically (via correspondent alliterative patterns), syntactically (via the subject – verb – direct object construction), and semantically (by the operation that links the non-human agent and the human vocal activity). Thus our experiment has produced a scrappet of humorous text, carefully layered:

Mr Brown's bull mastiff barracked the bread man; Mrs
Thompson's terrier taunted a passing tramp.

This small text offers a further possibility for manipulation, in the order of its two clauses. In the order given here, they present an attractive cadence, thanks to the epithet *passing*: *taunted a passing tramp*. It could be argued, however, that rhythmic strength should be sacrificed, in this instance, to a principle of semantic grading that places the more daring and unusual item second in a progression of licences. The reader is persuaded to accept the bold collocation of *terrier* and *taunted*, and having accepted it is prepared to accept the even bolder *bull mastiff – barracked*. The humorous tension is turned up a notch:

> Mrs Thompson's terrier taunted a passing tramp; Mr Brown's bull mastiff barracked the bread man.

Sometimes the progression from bold to bolder may be self-consciously marked by an adverbial intensifier:

> Mrs Thompson's terrier taunted a passing tramp, while Mr Brown's bull mastiff positively barracked the bread man.

Our exercise can be extended at will ('Write a paragraph on the theme "Hark, hark, the dogs do bark"'), with a few suggestions for further work:

> Mrs Dempster's Great Dane denounced the dustmen.
> Mrs Harris's hound harangued a hawker.
> Mr Carter's Corgi cursed all callers.

One possibility that might be investigated is that of modifying the text by revising the sound pattern. Humorous texts seldom exhibit such a thick studding of alliteration, particularly in continuous sequences; patterns are usually subtler, broken, less obtrusive, and of course it is possible for humorous language to dispense altogether with alliteration or any other form of phonetic marking. However, alliteration undoubtedly gives definition to the humorous design, and when it is completely avoided, as in the following example, the joke is muted:

> An officious chow taunted a passing vagrant; a lounging mastiff barracked the curate.

This revised text has its own quite strong pretensions to humour (*officious chow* and *lounging mastiff* call for investigation), but they are pretensions that do not include the bright rattle, the histrionic wink, of the alliterative phrase.

7.4 SETS AND SCALES

The 'sets' which the humorist, like any other creative writer, tries to exploit imaginatively, are somewhat inadequately represented in a thesaurus, where words are grouped in clusters expressing related motions. The inadequacy of the thesaurus is the fixity of its scope. A good thesaurus provides cross-references, showing how words may fall into more than one notional category, but still there is no book that can competently demonstrate the polysemic shifting of words as our thought locates and re-locates them in different groupings and perspectives. We labour with concepts like *synonym* (words of allied meaning), *antonym* (words of contrasted meaning), and *hyponym* (subordinate terms of a superordinate concept), and our cogitations yield an occasional glimpse of how these things might be interrelated, *eg*:

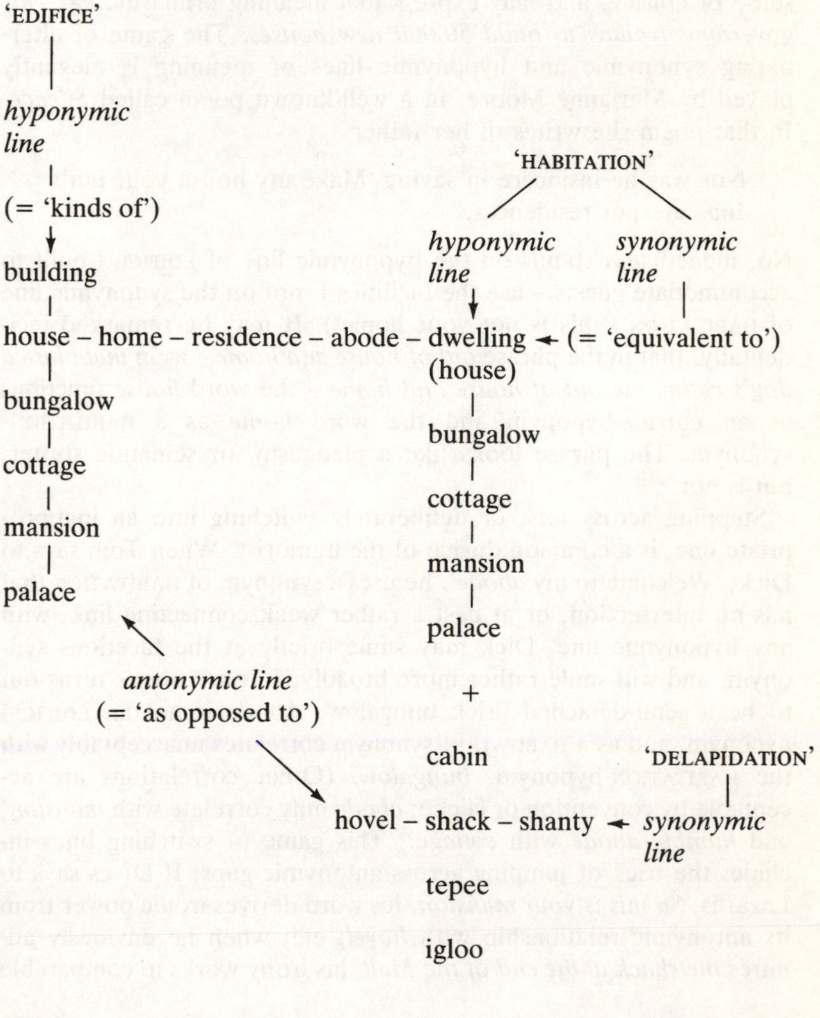

'EDIFICE'

hyponymic line

(= 'kinds of')

building

house – home – residence – abode – dwelling ← (= 'equivalent to')

bungalow

cottage

mansion

palace

antonymic line
(= 'as opposed to')

'HABITATION'

hyponymic line *synonymic line*

dwelling
(house)

bungalow

cottage

mansion

palace

+

cabin

hovel – shack – shanty ← *synonymic line*

'DELAPIDATION'

tepee

igloo

This presents in hypothetical outline a view of how large-scale notions (EDIFICE, HABITATION, *etc*) might be creatively explored, by following the intersecting 'lines' of words expressing types (hyponyms), equivalences (synonyms) and oppositions (antonyms). It suggests the importance of words like *house*, which stand, as it were, at the intersection of a synonymic and a hyponymic line. *House* carries the synonymic sense of HABITATION, and can be used exclusively or predominantly in that sense: *eg*: *He is master in his own house* (but not *He is master in his own bungalow*). It also carries the hyponymic sense of EDIFICE, and may express that meaning primarily: *eg*: *This government plans to build 50,000 new houses.* The game of alternating synonymic and hyponymic lines of meaning is elegantly played by Marianne Moore, in a well-known poem called *Silence*. In that poem she writes of her father:

> Nor was he insincere in saying 'Make my house your inn'.
> Inns are not residences.

No, indeed; *inn* stands on the hyponymic line of EDIFICE ('built to accommodate guests – use the facilities'), not on the synonymic line of HABITATION ('this is not your home'). It may be remarked incidentally, that in the phrase *out of house and home* – as in *that blasted dog's eating me out of house and home* – the word *house* functions as an EDIFICE-hyponym and the word *home* as a HABITATION-synonym. The phrase looks like a pleonasm, or semantic stutter; but is not.

Stepping across sets, or deliberately switching into an inappropriate line, is a common device of the humorist. When Tom says to Dick, 'Welcome to my *abode*', he uses a synonym of HABITATION that has no intersection, or at best a rather weak connecting link, with any hyponymic line. Dick may smile briefly at the facetious synonym, and will smile rather more broadly if Tom's *abode* turns out to be a semi-detached brick bungalow. *Abode* is not an EDIFICE-hyponym, and as a HABITATION-synonym correlates unacceptably with the HABITATION-hyponym, *bungalow*. (Other correlations are acceptable by convention or cliché; *abode* may correlate with *mansion*, and *humble abode* with *cottage*.) This game of switching lines includes the trick of jumping across antonymic gaps. If Dives says to Lazarus, *So this is your mansion*, his word derives ironic power from its antonymic relationship with *hovel*, etc; when he enviously admires *the shack at the end of the Mall*, his irony works in comparable fashion, as one of the synonyms of DELAPIDATION (*shack*) evokes an antonym (*palace*) on the hyponymic line of EDIFICE.

Such explanations of comic effect do not wholly illuminate the humorist's procedures. Is *abode* a potentially funny word merely because it is a comparatively rare synonym, felt to be rather pompous, and lacking the hyponymic linkages that more frequently attach to *dwelling* and *residence*? (Realtors may advertise the sale of handsome dwellings and stylish residences, but they never put *abodes* on the market.) This is a possible explanation, but it does not seem wholly adequate, and perhaps we should seek for other terms. Suppose, for example, that we were to assemble some words generally denoting 'dwelling place'; *eg*: *place*, *pad*, *house*, *abode*, *domicile*. An attempt to range these words along a scale with extremes of 'low formality' and 'high formality' might then produce this:

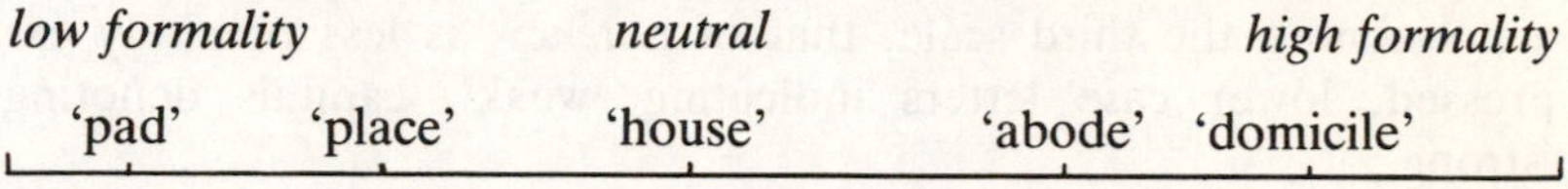

low formality *neutral* *high formality*

'pad' 'place' 'house' 'abode' 'domicile'

Formality here is essentially a social judgement on the propriety of discourse – 'appropriate to informal speech or writing', 'appropriate to general public usage', 'appropriate to the forms of literary or documentary convention', *etc*. On a *scale of formality*, slang words and colloquialisms like 'pad' and 'place' score low, whereas semi-archaic literary words like 'abode' or bureaucratic words like 'domicile' are assigned to the higher end. That 'house' is placed near the middle of the scale may be another way of presenting the intuition that this is a 'central' word, a nodal point in the web of meaning.

Scales can be devised for any pair of contrasting properties. (The idea of thus measuring a 'semantic differential' goes back to the work, in the 1950s, of the American psychologist Charles Osgood and his associates.) A *scale of evaluation*, for example, would invite assessments of *good* and *bad*:

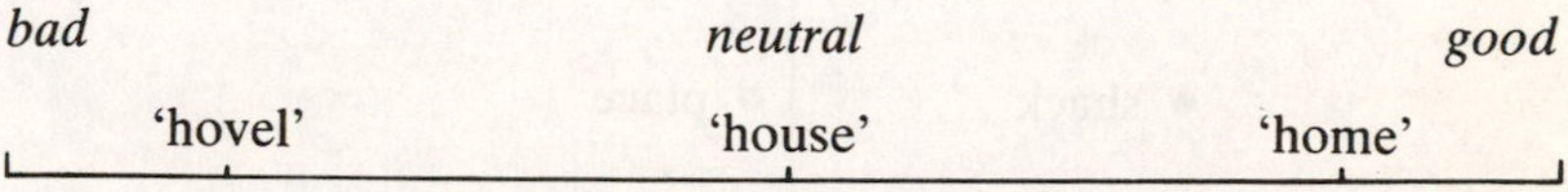

bad *neutral* *good*

'hovel' 'house' 'home'

The relationship of 'house' to 'home' is presented here in terms different from, but not incompatible with, those suggested earlier.

Here it is not a question of allotting a word to a set, but rather of ascribing to it a value, or an affective response. Thus when we say that 'home' *means more* than 'house', it is this affective value we have in mind.

A companion measure assesses the strength of affective responses, on a *scale of potency*:

weak	*neutral*	*strong*
'domicile', 'place'	'house'	'hovel', 'home'

What Osgood has called the 'semantic space' defined coordinately by two or more scales is illustrated in the diagram below. The scale of *formality* forms the vertical axis, the scale of *evaluation* makes a horizontal; the third scale, that of *potency*, is less precisely expressed, lower case letters indicating 'weak', capitals denoting 'strong':

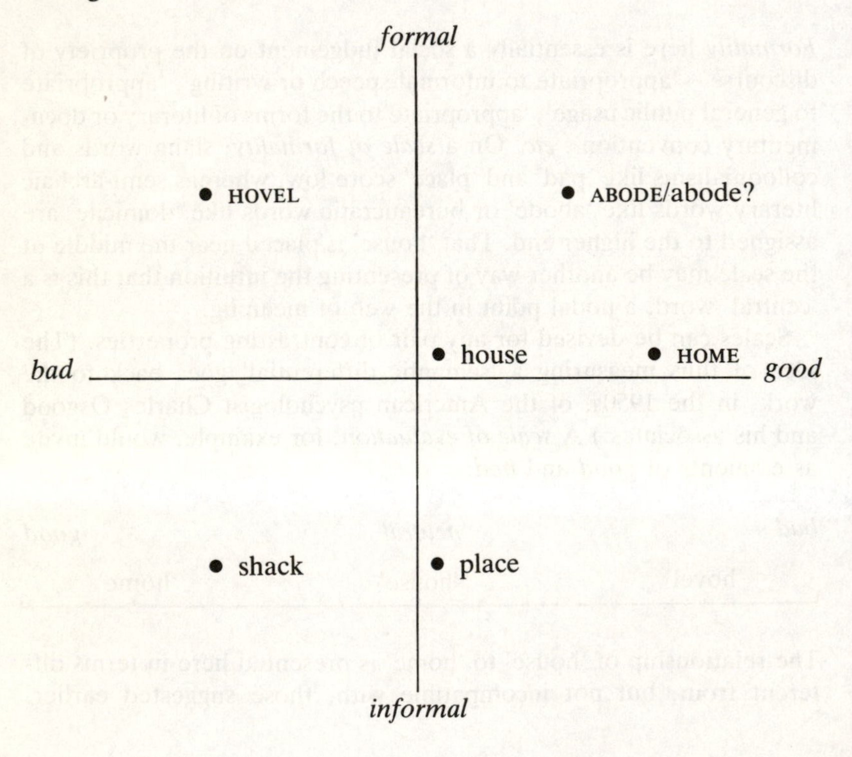

One person's assessments are plotted here. On this measure, *abode* is clearly 'formal' and 'good', but there is some uncertainty about its strength. Its poetic contexts suggest that it ought to be residually *strong*:

> No farther seek his merits to disclose
>   Or draw his frailties from their dread abode,
> (There they alike in trembling hope repose,)
>   The bosom of his Father and his God.

Gray's lines remind us that an abode is no mere residence; it is a place where one *abides* – in this case, for all eternity. To characterize *abode* as 'strong' is to explain in part the facetious humour of remarks like *What say we toddle down to my humble abode for drinkies*? Into a context of low formality and rather weak affective power is introduced, with incongruous effect, a highly formal word strongly connotative of security, permanence, possibly of quasi-religious solemnity. This kind of play, along 'scalar' axes, characterizes many humorous formulations: *Shall we proceed to my pad for a spot of liquid refreshment*?; *Let us sally forth to my domicile and imbibe a few snorts*; *We'll trek to my shack and put a few back*; *Haste with locomotive zeal to yon mansion, where possets of fermented liquor shall be our portion*; *Let's skedaddle to my seat and rape the grape*; *Leg it, lads, to my residence, where the bonny booze awaits*; *We'll push off to poppa's palace and ingurgitate the odd potation*. The game of whimsy is so easy if one knows the simple rules of set and scale.

7.5 PUNS RULE; THE SPUN LURE

The management of humorous language is largely a matter of devising transfers – the transfer from set to set, from scale to scale, from layer to layer, until the happy confusion of a double vision is achieved. At the heart of this process of continual and multiple transference, an important process aping the shiftiness of thought itself, is the apparently frivolous device of the pun; word-play is the lure, the spinning toy, that draws up the lurking and fishy meaning. We take punning for a tawdry and facetious thing, one of the less profound forms of humour, but that is the prejudice of our time; a pun may be profoundly serious, or charged with pathos. We also take it for a simple thing, which it is not; a typology of punning would occupy many pages and catalogue many variants. What follows is not an attempt to list exhaustively the modes of the pun, but a general commentary on some prominent types:

(a) Homophones

Homophones are pairs (or more) of words having the same sound but different meanings, *eg*: *rain/reign*, *sighs/size*, *urn/earn*, *need/knead*. The difference of meaning is reflected in distinctive spellings. Many riddles turn on homophonic puns:

> When does the baker follow his trade?
> – Whenever he needs (kneads)
>
> or
>
> When does the baker follow his trade?
> – Whenever he needs (kneads) the dough.

The second version adds to the homophonic pun on *needs/kneads* a homonymic play on *dough*, which means (i) 'flour-and-water paste', (ii) 'money'. (On *homonyms*, see (f) below.)

The homophonic pun is the form above all loved and practised by nineteenth-century wits like Lamb and Hood and Carroll. The Victorian era, indeed, is sometimes blamed for bringing the pun into intellectual disrepute, as a mere exercise in parlour jocosity; though homophonic skittishness had already enjoyed one outrageous run, in Tudor times. The plays of Shakespeare – comedies, histories, and tragedies alike – are littered with homophonic quibbles, very often of obscene import. A typical sample is the seemingly innocuous phrase *and thereby hangs a tale*. (See *As You Like It*, II. VII. 26; the lines concluding with this phrase are among the most nastily prurient in the canon, but time has wheedled them into innocence.) The point of this pawky piece of Tudor rudery is the homophony of *tale* and *tail*, which entails (*mea culpa*) the double meaning of 'caudal appendage' and 'penis'. A more respectable example of the Shakespearean obsession with punning is the tiresome bandying of *all* and *awl* in the first scene of *Julius Caesar*. The cobbler, who lives by his awl and all, tells the tribune he plies a very honourable trade, as a mender of soles/souls.

(b) Homophonic phrases

There are rare instances of phrasal homophony: syllable for syllable, phrases sound alike, but the sum of the meaning is different. Unlike homophonic words, they are not readily available in the stock of the language. Phrasal homophony has to be forced, as the following example shows:

> Where did Humpty Dumpty leave his hat?
> – Humpty dumped 'is 'at on a wall.

The word-play of the riddling answer, which puns with elaborate homophony on the nursery-rhyme line *Humpty Dumpty sat on a wall*, requires the phonetics of non-standard English. It would go well enough in West Ham or Nottingham, but perhaps not so certainly in Hampstead. A further constraint on the homophonic phrase may be the rhythm and stress-timing of English. French, with its syllable-timing, possibly creates more favourable conditions for phrasal homophony.

(c) Mimes

'Mimes' (a nonce-term) are phonetic similitudes, usually rhymes, with the appeal of homophones. They make for a particularly outrageous kind of pun, because they bend the rules of punning itself, bending the bender, as it were. The central principle of punning is *homomorphic* ('homomorph' = 'the same form'), but mimes are impudently *allomorphic* ('allomorph' = 'variant form'). An example, from the primary school treasury:

> What do policemen have in their sandwiches?
> – Truncheon meat.

What *truncheon* impishly mimes is obviously the word *luncheon*. Another example, from the same copious source:

> What do cats read?
> – The Mews of the World.

In which oracle, *mews* mimes *news*. The pun is deeper than one might at first suppose, since it links the notion of 'vocalizing', 'phonation', 'oral activity', with that of 'publicizing', 'announcing', 'proclaiming'. (The same combination of the notions 'sound' and

'publicity' is evident in the names of some newspapers, *eg*: *The Echo*, *The Clarion*.)
Two further examples, with a minimum of comment:

> What did the duck say as it flew upside down?
> – I'm quacking up.

To this there is a companion joke, an amazing wisequack:

> What language is quack-quack?
> – Double ducks.

This mime (*ducks/Dutch*) lacks even the excuse of rhyming.

(d) Mimetic phrases

The diner, scanning the menu, says *I see you serve cod and salmon*, challenging the waiter to recognize his adroit mimicry of the Biblical injunction (Matthew vi, 24), *Ye cannot serve God and mammon*. Such mimetic phrasing is a staple of wit, and generally reflects the humorist's reading in primary texts (the Bible, Shakespeare), his command of literary phraseology, his repertoire of slogans:

> Hollywood, land of mink and money.
> (mimetic of the Biblical 'land of milk and honey')
> What food these mortals eat.
> (This is James Thurber's invention. He imagines a time when dolphins have become the master species, and man a mere laboratory animal. Observing humans at table, the dolphins say *what food these mortals eat* – miming Puck's *Lord, what fools these mortals be*)

A children's book has a vignette of two bees, one of whom, masked and pistolled, is saying to the other *Your honey or your life*. The phrase 'your money or your life' is also mimicked in the joke about the desperado who bursts into a restaurant, intent on relieving the well-heeled diners of their valuables, but is so taken by the youth and beauty of one lady that he turns to her portly, middle-aged escort and enquires: *Your honey – or your wife*?

(e) Homonyms

The homonym is a companion device to the homophone:

For her pleasure, Auntie Joan
  Played the crooning homophone,
Accompanied by Uncle Jim
  On the wheezing homonym.

Homonyms share a spelling and split a meaning: *wheeze* = (i) breathe with squeaky, puffing sound, (ii) noun (theatrical slang) a joke interpolated by the actor during a performance; *school* = (i) 'educational establishment', (ii) 'collection of fish'; *dough* = (i) 'flour paste', (ii) (slang) 'money'; *run* = (i) verb, denoting a mode of human locomotion, (ii) verb, denoting a process (non-human) of extending. Homonymic puns are common, and mostly corny:

Where do fish learn to swim?
– In a school.

(Carroll elaborates this joke through four pun-laden pages in Ch. IX of *Alice in Wonderland* – the Mock Turtle episode)

What runs along every street in town?
– The pavement.

(This is a culturally-conditioned joke. It would have to be revised for use in America, where *pavement* customarily refers to the surface, or 'metalling' of the actual road, and the equivalent of British 'pavement' is *sidewalk*)

One or two essays in the genre show greater subtlety:

How do you get down from an elephant?
– You don't. You get down from a swan.

This is a sophisticated quip, imposing homonymic identity on two distinct constructions of the verb: *get down* = phrasal verb, 'descend', and *get/down* = verb + object, 'obtain this commodity, *ie* swansdown'.

(f) Homonymic phrases

Whole phrases can be turned into homonymic puns. This, indeed, is a common procedure in making 'tag' jokes (see §3.6(d)):

'I have designs on you', as the tattooist said to his girl.

The idiom *to have designs on* = 'to have plans for conquest or acquisition'; so that 'I have designs on you' means, in the language of romance, 'I intend to make you mine.' Here, however, a second meaning is forced. *I have designs on you* = 'I have tattooed you'. The homonymic phrase is greatly favoured by skittish sub-editors composing newspaper headlines:

Winning candidate out for the count.

This referred to an election in which the winner had gone home, exhausted, before the votes were finally tallied. *The count* = 'process of tallying votes in an election'; *out for the count* = 'unconscious' (*ie* during the boxing referee's count of ten); thus, while the votes were being counted the winner was out for the count.

(g) Contacts and Blends

Some turns of phrase echo other idioms and take a colour of meaning from them; there is a casual contact of ideas, or a blending of semantic components. For instance, a colleague invited to comment on a student's dissertation writes to me that the candidate seems to have *read around in linguistics*. If I understand this as a covertly sardonic observation, it is because *read around* evokes *sleep around*, and a proportion is thereby established between the meanings 'sleep with a lot of partners, without emotional commitment', and 'consult a lot of books, without intellectual discipline'. My student, it appears, has not 'read deeply' in linguistics; he has *read around – ie* read superficially, with meretricious intent.

This is an example of a very subtle kind of punning. A judgement is conveyed here, in ostensibly neutral or even favourable language, which, however, suggests *contact* with another, less innocuous phrase. An instance of what might be called a *blend, ie* a more readily apparent invasion of one phrase by another, would be the expression *a proposition of a different colour*. This is a sort of idiomatic portmanteau. (On 'portmanteau', see (i) below.) One construction, *a proposition of a different kind* carries the sense, as it were, of the message; the lurking, incursive idiom, *a horse of a different colour*, infuses an element of judgement or evaluation (approval, assessment of form, *etc.*) Some blends are knowingly devised; others are sheer malapropisms. Thurber reports an acquaintance as saying, of a legal dispute, *So they decided to leave it where sleeping dogs lie* – a wonderfully malaproposed blend of *let sleeping dogs lie* and *leave it where it lies*.

(h) Pseudomorphs

Behold the silly pseudomorph, flexing its unmuscles:

Samson was terribly distressed by Delilah.

Distressed because *dis-tressed*; shorn therefore forlorn. There is no verb *to dis-tress* in English; it is a false form, a pseudomorph, invented to make a homonymic pun. Prefixes like *dis-* and *ex-* lend themselves to the game:

A: In his exposition, he took a very firm stand on spending cuts.
B: How can you stand in an ex-position?

But any word with an arbitrarily detachable pseudo-morpheme will also serve:

What do you do with a wombat?
– Play wom.

(i) Portmanteaux

Lewis Carroll gave us the term *portmanteau* – gave in jest what is now used in terminological earnest – as a label for the coinage that packs two meanings into one word. In *Through The Looking Glass*, Humpty Dumpty – linguist, philosopher and exegete – comments on the strange poem called 'Jabberwocky', and explains to Alice that words like *slithy* and *mimsy* are portmanteaux, *ie* of 'lithe' and 'slimy' in the one case and 'flimsy' and 'miserable' in the other. Portmanteaux now travel widely, in literature (see *Finnegan's Wake*), in comic patter, in youthful riddles:

If buttercups are yellow, what colour are hiccups?
– Burple

And also, we might add, in divers tongues – *eg* the following stately and sonorous portmanteau-pun, made by a Swedish student, who referred to a well-known actress – regal of bearing, generous in personality, generous, too, in her physical endowments – as *barmhertiginnan*. This was a brilliant composition of the following elements:

barm	= 'bosom'
barmhertig	= 'merciful', 'gracious'
hertiginna	= 'duchess'
-n	= the definite article

Thus, *barmhertiginnan* expresses the combined notions of 'bosominess', 'graciousness', and 'nobility of style'. A pun of Joycean dimensions, it is nurtured by what used to be called 'the genius of the language'; Swedish permits quite readily the formation of elaborate compounds, and its poetry is rich in them.

(j) Etymological puns

There is a scholarly kind of punning that pleases itself, and any attentive observer, with sly reflections on the etymology of words, thus:

> Nero made Rome the focus of his artistic attention.

The buried joke here is that *focus* in Latin has the meaning 'hearth', or 'fireplace'; Nero, fiddling while Rome burned, had the whole city in focus. Such jokes are both arch and arcane, and the maker of them must be prepared, like the perpetrator of the following, to spend a lot of time giggling to himself:

A	(sentimentally commenting on a rural scene):	'"The ploughman homeward plods his weary way"'
B	(grave):	'He must be tired.'
C	(impish):	'He's obviously delirious.'

This joke was doomed to misfire; *C* was obliged to explain, and apologize. For why should *A* and *B* be expected to have at first hand the knowledge that *delirious* means, etymologically, 'out of the furrow' – which, indeed, is where the weary ploughman is when he has finished his ploughing? As a social footnote, it may be remarked that etymological puns are often coldly, even angrily received, being regarded as pretentious and undemocratic. If they seem to be a form of pedantic humour peculiarly favoured by English, this is perhaps because much of our vocabulary, especially in literature and learning, consists of classical derivatives which are etymologically 'opaque' to anyone who has no smattering of Latin or Greek. This facilitates a snobbery in joking; the play on *focus* is a coterie quip, for those in the know. By contrast, we may consider German, where the same joke could be made, using the word *Brennpunkt* (literally and obviously 'burning point'); but then the pun would be overt, whereas the charm of the pun on *focus* is its covert, audience-defining character.

(k) Bilingual puns

The bilingual pun is another demonstration of cute pedantry, often, however, occurring in an explanatory context that permits the uninitiated to see the point. The essence of the bilingual joke is that a foreign word is made to bear the sense of an English word, whether by homophonic accident, by homonymic/semantic contrivance (*eg* Swift's play on *Mantua* and *Cremona*), or by literal translation. Third-form vaudevillians will have no difficulty with the bilingual pun in the following mock epitaph, one of the 'little Willie' family of jokes;

> Here lies Willie Longbottom Aged 6
> *-Ars longa, vita brevis-*

But this is fundamentally designed for British ears; the pun on *ars* does not sit so well in American English. A better example of bilingual punning is supplied by the following snippet of dinner-table conversation. A guest remarked on the vivacity and prettiness of one of the waitresses:

A: That's a dolly bird! Eh?
B: I believe she comes from the Seychelles.
C: Aha! A Seychelloise.
D: A Seychelloiseau.

The pun is prepared and underpinned by its conversational scaffolding: *bird* = 'woman'; 'woman from the Seychelles' = *Seychelloise* – *B* makes the skip from English to French; *oise* invites, associatively, *oiseau*; *oiseau* = 'bird'. On this occasion, *D* took his chance with a grateful avidity that recalls Thurber's story of having been mistaken for Bing Crosby at a bibulous party:

> '*Non sum qualis eram sub regno bony Sinatra*', I said quickly, having waited for years to wedge that line in somewhere.
> 'You finally made it,' my wife said, for she knows all my lines, wedged and unwedged.

Thurber puns on the name of the (once) gaunt-cheeked singer, Frank Sinatra, and on that of Cinara, one of Horace's literary loves, celebrated in *Odes*, IV, 1: *Non sum qualis eram bonae sub regno Cinarae*, 'I am not what I was when dear Cinara ruled my heart'.

(l) Pun–metaphors

A frisky trick of journalism is the headline that shakes a cliché to rattle a metaphor to ring a pun:

Council puts brake on progress of cycle path scheme.
Murky consequences of washing our hands of Europe.

The second example (from the *Guardian*) illustrates the ramshackle character of this variety of punning. A poetic metaphor is precise, and in its precision illuminating. Pun-metaphors are often deliberately sloppy. To *wash one's hands*, as Pontius Pilate demonstrated, is to absolve oneself of responsibility; but the headline writer does not really want to use the phrase in that sense. His latent verb is not 'abnegate', 'repudiate', or 'disavow', but quite simply 'withdraw from'; what he is referring to is the possibility of Britain's withdrawal from the European Economic Community. His casual use of the hand-washing idiom, however, enables him to work the pun on *murky*, using a figurative meaning, 'disreputable', side by side with its primary meaning, 'dark', here stretched to include the nuance 'dirty'. This freedom with the dictionary admits the creation of a kind of oxymoron, the suggestion of a dirty cleanliness. In literal fact we 'wash our hands' to be rid of dirt; but the kind of hand-washing the headline writer denotes can have no clean issue.

This catalogue of pun-types may well be capable of extension, for the activity of punning, so often deplored, is widespread and is practised even by its accusers. Puns, like metaphors, fossilize in the very substance of the language; it is hardly possible to work the ground extensively without turning up a figure or a pun. At the heart of all this word-play seems to be a concern with two ancient and related processes: naming and riddling. So often, in folklore, to know a name, a secret name, is to have power, but the power can only be secured by the adept who guesses the answer to a riddle. In the most preposterous riddles of the playground there lurks this traditional sense, of being compelled, like the wise scribes of old, to find the right name, the power-giving name:

What's a myth?
– A female moth.

The anonymous author of this riddle may not have been aware of doing anything profound with language; it has the air of plain high-spirited lunacy. But the lisping adroitness of the mime-pun on *myth/miss*, and, even more, the reminder that vowel gradation characterizes some grammatical and lexical distinctions in English (number, in *foot/feet*, tense in *ring/rang*, sex, in *fox/vix*(en), age, in *cat/kit*(ten)) imply linguistic competence of no small order. And it is ludicrously and temporarily convincing; like all humour it commands its moment of absolute surrender. If *myth* is not the name for a female moth, our creative fantasy tells us, it *ought* to be. What is additionally funny about this riddle is its confident implication (a) that there exists a word denoting 'female moth', and (b) that we have need of the word. Alas, our studies and our common transactions discover no need for it; but the spirit of humour can always defend itself in King Lear's words – *O! reason not the need; our basest beggars are in the poorest things superfluous*.

7.6 GRAPHOLOGIES: O, MAN'S GREAT GAMES – GET SOME ANAGRAMS

There are visual equivalents to the pun in various forms of graphological trick: freak typography, acrostics, the rebus, the palindrome (*madam, I'm Adam*), the anagram. Among these, it is the latter that most evidently possesses something of the sweet serendipity of punning. Just as a pun may happily nudge us into the perception of some latent nuance of meaning, so anagrams may suggest connections hitherto unperceived. An anagram is a free play with a limited set of letters, the working of a comic Ouija board in the hope of making contact with the ghost of a joke. Let us say that I attempt an anagram on my name, Walter Nash. Without too much trouble I am able to rearrange the constituent letters so as to read *Ah, stern law*, or *Al wants her*, or *Wash later, N*. Not very remarkable, perhaps, but I can use at least one of these to frame a gentle witticism:

Ah, stern law, that I am Walter Nash.

Note first of all the secretive nature – the exclusiveness, almost – of this humour. There is a code to be broken. A reader given no forewarning of the anagram would have to be alert enough to perceive in that odd phrase 'Ah, stern law', the sign of an *intention of joke*; and hence to proceed to break the code. This challenge to the perceptions is, as we have noted, a feature of certain types of pun; puns and anagrams represent an element of code-breaking in humour. The anagram presents a further analogy, in its affinity with the semantic processes of rhyme. Rhymes, through their coincidences of sound, suggest associations of meaning; *eg* fairly obviously, *blame* and *shame* ('accusation' – 'response to accusation'), or, somewhat more remotely, *shiver* and *liver* (?'symptom' – 'source of complaint'?), or, more remotely still, *founder* and *surround her* (?? 'important figure' – / courtiers, sycophants, officials / 'entourage'??).

An anagram can be seen as a kind of semantic matching expressed in letters instead of sounds, the re-patterned phrase suggesting some arbitrary but momentarily convincing link with the original. Thus, *Ah, stern law, that I am Walter Nash* is an 'anagrammatic rhyme'. As to its meaning, it might be interpreted as a humorous variation on a determinist theme: 'We are what nature makes us. Oh, how I often wish it were otherwise, but there you are, that's destiny. Take me as you find me. I can't help it.' It is certainly not easy to impose any such unifying construction on *Walter Nash* + *Al wants her*, or *Walter Nash* + *Wash later, N*, but then it might be argued that *Al wants her* and *Wash later, N* are 'remote' anagrams, comparable to 'remote' rhymes, requiring the formation of a fairly elaborate connective chain of implied meanings.

Two sections of this chapter are headed by anagrams. One of them (*o, man's great games – get some anagrams*) is no more than a piece of playful decoration. The other (*puns rule – spun lure*) is more ambitious, and is worth dwelling on for a moment because it illustrates not only how anagrams work but also how the mind plays creatively with rags of language and tatters of experience. The phrase *puns rule* echoes a motif from an earlier chapter (the 'OK' jokes discussed in Ch. 4.1). When this is transformed into *spun lure*, the 'anagrammatic rhyme' may seem so remote as to exclude much possibility of meaningful association. But the possibility exists, and, indeed, is declared in the words *word play is the lure, the spinning toy that draws up the lurking and fishy meaning* (see p. 137). The intended allusion is to the spoon-shaped piece of bright metal which the fisherman puts on a spinner and pays out behind his boat. Recollections from boyhood of fishing on Lake Windermere, and specifically of trolling for pike, furnish the *personal* (as against the *textual*) source of the anagram; I remember the excitement of the strike, and the exhilaration, half-fearful, as a particularly strong fish actually began to run away with the skiff. In later years, such experiences are accommodated to literary convention, as images for the darkness of the mind, the search for meaning, the joy of discovery. Consider, then, what happens at that point in our text where – casually, it seems – the anagram *puns rule/spun lure* is formed. It is not so casual. The word-play has a textual origin, in a motif discussed many pages earlier. Without that precedent discussion, the phrase *puns rule* might seem as meaningless as a name without a denotation. Reference to the continuing textual process is necessary before we can understand *puns rule* as the anagrammatic base of *spun lure*. Once that base is established, the creative anagram, the 're-literation' that humorously suggests a semantic relationship, an explanatory metaphor, a representative image, becomes possible. *Spun lure – puns rule* may not be especially funny, and was not in any case designed to provoke laughter; but it does say something about the ecology and creative impulses of humour.

7.7 LUCKY LAPSES

On the other hand, there are formulations that have no design and no creative history; lucky lapses; examples of the comic *felix culpa* which could not be improved by taking thought. Often the originators of these are people whose conceptual reach slightly exceeds their linguistic grasp; who know well enough what they want to say, but through ignorance, or failure of memory, through some neurophysiological defect, or even through sheer pretentiousness, cannot quite manage to say it. Some of these tumblers in language achieve name and fame – *eg* the luckless Revd William Archibald (*I'll-damn-you-for-sewages*) Spooner, who is said to have dismissed a student with the words *You have deliberately tasted two worms and you can leave Oxford by the town drain*; and the great Sam Goldwyn, who has enriched the English language with such delightful pronouncements as *Include me out* and *In two words: im-possible*. Historically, the type of the linguistic blunderer is celebrated in fictional characters like Dogberry (*Comparisons are odorous*) and Mrs Malaprop (*If I reprehend anything in this world, it is the use of my oracular tongue, and a nice derangement of epitaphs*).

In such cases, the propensity to error is a kind of malady, which we label with the suffix-*ism*; we speak of Spoonerisms, Goldwynisms, Malapropisms. Some patients, however, are not above the suspicion of cunningly reproducing and marketing their own symptoms, or of encouraging others to do so (it is sometimes said that Sam Goldwyn knew perfectly well what he was doing). There is a type of designed humour that seizes on the possibilities of innocent error. Take, for example, the humour of ambiguity. Some ambiguities are merely hapless howlers, *eg* the case of the shopkeeper who advertised in her local paper that *Mrs X has cast off clothing of all descriptions, and invites inspection*, or that of the memorial *erected to the memory of James Macmillan, drowned in the Severn by some of his closest friends*. These untutored instances remind us that English has syntactic snares that can be artfully sprung:

> Would you rather an elephant attacked you or a gorilla?
> – I'd rather he attacked the gorilla.

A further source of haphazard humour is the typographical error. James Thurber provides the following instances:

> There's no business like shoe business.
> The gates of Hell shall now prevail.
> A stitch in time saves none.

The happiness of literal errors like these is that the misplacing of one small letter completely subverts or gainsays the sense of an assertion. The proverb *A stitch in time saves nine* is a precautionary wisdom, the force of which is rudely negated when *nine* is misprinted as *none*. A funny misprint is thus a casual invitation to irreverence. The subversive humour of the literal error is the point of an academic joke that once circulated in the Senior Common Room at a certain British university. On the retirement of an eminent Vice Chancellor, the Senate commissioned a portrait bust, on the plinth of which was to be inscribed the words *Invenit collegium*, *reliquit universitatem*, 'He found a college; he left a university'. Unfortunately, the craftsman entrusted with the carving and gilding of the inscription made a small mistake, and when the bust was unveiled its message was seen to read *Invenit collegam, reliquit universitatem*, which classical wits promptly translated 'He found a female colleague and quit the university'.

Mistranslations (excessively literal or misguidedly ambitious) are a fine source of the unconscious humour that can be worked into conscious designs. An Italian coffee percolator that I once owned came with a set of instructions in English, including the strange injunction to *set on fire and abide the ejaculation*. The beauty of such aberrations is that while the meaning is reasonably clear, it is expressed in language so far removed from standard idiom as to constitute an exotic strain of poetry. It was the perception of such potential in the language of a tourist pamphlet that led Robert Graves to write a very funny poem called '*!Wellcome, To The Caves of Arta!*' He prefaces his poem with a passage from the leaflet:

> They are hollowed out in the see coast at the muncipal terminal of Capdepera, at nine kilometer from the town of Arta in the Island of Mallorca, with a suporizing infinity of graceful colums of 21 meter and by downward, wich prives the spectator of all animacion and plunges in dumbness. The way going is very picturesque, serpentine between style mountains, til the arrival at the esplanade of the vallee called 'The Spider'. There are good enlacements of the railroad with autobuses of excursion, many days of the week, today actually Wednesday and Satturday Since many centuries renown foreing visitors have explored them and wrote their eulogy about, included Nort-American geoglogues.

And his poem begins:

> Such subtile filigranity and nobless of construccion
> Here fraternise in harmony, that respiracion stops.
> While all admit their impotence (though autors most formidable)
> To sing in words the excellence of Nature's underprops,
> Yet stalactite and stalagmite together with dumb language
> Make hymnes to God wich celebrate the stregnth of water drops. [13]

Mrs Malaprop would doubtless have applauded this, as a very nice derangement of epitaphs in the oracular tongue. What may be noted, is that neither in the stanza quoted nor in the rest of his poem does Graves refer directly, in the form of any identifiable citation, to his pamphlet-source. It is stimulus rather than source; from its varieties of error he generates a comic/poetic dialect. Thus mistakes have their heuristic value; through them we may discover paradoxes, epigrams, metaphors, ironies, singularly beautiful and grotesque forms of humour, sculpted by chance usage like pieces of wood on the beach.

7.8 IRONIES

As to irony, indisputably a major stylistic resort in humour, it is difficult to find clear definitions and concise accounts of its workings; particularly since literary critics are in the habit of using the word to denote any oblique reflection, any inconsistency of character, any unforeseen turn in the fable, any sign of a perverse current of meaning not directed by the author. If these things are ironic, then literature thrives on irony; but the word then loses much of its technical content and becomes, like 'beauty' or 'elegance', an affective label. Dictionaries and books of reference are a little uneasy about its narrower import, as denoting a type of linguistic usage. The consensus appears to be this: that the ironist insincerely states something he does not mean, but through the manner of his statement – whether through its formulation, or its delivery, or both – is able to encode a counter-proposition, his 'real meaning', which may be interpreted by the attentive listener or reader. Irony is generally said to differ from sarcasm in this particular, that the sarcastic statement is ostensibly sincere, though it, too, is coded with some mark of peculiar emphasis. Following these guidelines, we may attempt to encode sarcastic and ironic expressions of the proposition *Tommy is lazy*. Sarcastically, it might be said that *Tommy doesn't strain himself*; ironically, that *Tommy is renowned for his labours*.

The coding is the key to the distinction. Sarcasm uses a *pro-code*, that is, a form of words ostensibly equivalent in denotation to the parent proposition. Thus *Tommy doesn't strain himself*, or *Tommy likes to take it easy*, or *Tommy believes in working at a leisurely pace* may be offered as tantamount to *Tommy is lazy*. They cannot be wholly tantamount, however, because apart from any consideration of philosophical entailments, the *pro-code* must involve a pejorative *counter-code*, expressing the speaker's unsympathetic or hostile attitude. This counter-code may take the form of a fulsome intonation and vocal timbre ('*Poor chap*! *He must be tired*! *What a shame*!) or may depend on the operation of understatement and overstatement. '*Dear me! Tommy's scratched his pinky*!' and '*Send for Dr Kildare! Thomas has lacerated his digit*!' might be examples respectively of sarcastic understatement and sarcastic overstatement, in relationship to the observation *Tommy has cut his little finger*. A negative formulation complicates the procedure by converting into understatement the implication of overstatement. Thus *He strains himself* overstates *He is hard-working*; but *He doesn't strain himself* is perceived as a sarcastic understatement of *He is lazy*.

Irony *mal-codes*, designedly choosing forms of words that misrepresent the content of the message. I wish to say that *Tommy is lazy*; I declare that *Tommy is renowned for his labours*, compounding my falsehood, if I choose, by the addition of ponderous modifiers, *eg* '*vastly* renowned', '*prodigious* labours'. These strokes of hyperbole are part of the process of counter-coding which irony also requires, though the ironic counter-code is not, like that of sarcasm, a means of emphasizing an attitude, but rather, a matter of reversing significances. In this instance, the counter-coding to which a recipient of the message is invited to respond is in the overstatement of *renowned*, *vastly*, *prodigious*. An understating counter-code would be equally possible (*eg*: *Tommy lifts the occasional finger*, *Say 'Tommy' and you have almost said 'effort'*); and in spoken communication irony may be additionally coded by a tone of voice, a special intonation, tempo, and timbre identifiable within the confines of a certain speech-community.

Perhaps the most important concomitant of the ironic utterance, however, is the existence of acknowledged facts and accepted attitudes that provide a kind of 'truth condition' for whatever is proposed. To have referred, in the year 1940, to *Adolf Hitler, noted benefactor of mankind*, would have been, as far as the inhabitants of Britain and most of Europe were concerned, an outrageous irony; but in Germany it would have been accepted (necessarily) at its face value. It is always possible for irony to fail transactionally, because the recipient is ignorant of, or does not acknowledge, the suppositions underlying the message. There is also a risk of failure in fine irony, when the ironist so hones and reduces the features of counter-coding that the recipient is at times led to wonder whether the message is, after all, seriously intended and formulated. Irony is a vulnerable mode of humorous composition, partly because of these risks and partly because long passages of ironic writing weary and discompose the reader, suggesting in the end a morbid rather than a healthily humorous spirit.

These reflections are based on the assumption that the irony/sarcasm distinction, as formulated in dictionaries, glossaries, *etc*, is necessary and wholly valid. There may be some doubt about this. Both sarcasm and irony are counter-coded, and it is in the counter-coding that puzzling affinities are often seen. If I say *He doesn't strain himself, does he*?, with a certain intonation, I am sarcastic. But what if I say, with the same sardonic intent and the same kind of intonation, *He strains himself, doesn't he*? Is this still sarcasm? Or am I now operating the ironic counter-code? If I declare that *Tommy doesn't believe in overdoing it*, what does the counter-code imply? Sarcastic mockery? (= 'Tommy is idle'); or ironic understatement? (= 'Tommy in fact gets through an impressive amount of work') The context – knowledge of Tommy and his doings – would supply our answer; but the coding is ambiguous.

A further difficulty is the possibility of confusing the ironic with the merely oblique. I enquire of a friend, *Are you well*?, and he replies *As well as my doctor expects me to be*, with a slight variation on the conventional *As well as can be expected*. Because of this small but noticeable peculiarity of formulation, I am momentarily at a loss to know whether this reply is a gently jocose periphrasis meaning 'Fairly well', or an ironic onslaught on the medico – 'My doctor thinks I'm well, but then how would *he* know, the incompetent quack?; if you really want to know, I feel ghastly.' As our conversation unfolds, this uncertainty is resolved; but the instance does illustrate the fact that irony, which we commonly assume to be a lucid, perspicuous form of wit, a philosopher's vehicle almost, can be so elusively presented as to be quite opaque.

Ambiguities, ambivalences, the couplings and contrasts of meaning, all characterize the exploratory and creative procedures of humorous language. The humorist tries by every means in his power to elicit from the system of language potential significances, co-significances, counter-significances, the play of values, the coincidences or oppositions of points in a network of choices. This exploitation of dualities inherent in resources and usage is one important aspect of language in its humour, but it is not the whole account of the subject; there remains the matter of language as a stage for humorous recitals.

Eight

Language in its humour: (ii) the staging of recitals

8.1 RHYME AND RHYTHM

Humour has its prosodic laws that command the resources (alliteration, rhyme, rhythm) but flout the principles of 'serious' poetics. In comic versifying, rhyme and rhythm have, potentially, a dual function. We may regard them as merely decorative applications, providing a setting and, so to speak, a lighting for the humour, or we may assign to them a more significant role as directive elements, features that organize the comedy and are essential to it. In this, comic verse is not so different from any other kind of verse composition; lyric poetry also uses rhyme and rhythm both decoratively and directively. The subversiveness of humorous prosody, however, lies in its whimsical play with the notions of expectation and probability – with the game of prediction. The following notes elaborate this theme.

(a) Predicting the rhyme

Comic rhymes are effective either because they are banal and easily predictable, or because they are so remote as to defy expectation. Two rhyming styles are implied here, and mastery of both is exemplified in the work of the Victorian scholar and wit C.S. Calverley. Calverley had a flair for delicately-rhythmed strophic forms, through which banal masculine (monosyllabic) rhymes would trudge on flattened feet:

> The sports, to which with boyish glee
>   I sprang erewhile, attract no more;
> Although I am but sixty-three
>   Or four.
> Nay, worse than that, I've seemed of late

To shrink from happy boyhood – boys
Have grown so noisy, and I hate
A noise. [4; *pp* 65–6]

One of the pleasures of four-square rhyming in this style is the ease with which the reader can anticipate the rhyming word, waiting for its arrival across the artfully-timed suspensions of the metre. Prediction is supported by clues in the text; for example, the occurrence of the word *noisy* in the penultimate line promotes the expectation that the rhyme for *boys* will be *noise*.

By contrast, Calverley's feminine (disyllabic) rhymes create sharp moments of surprise:

I love to gaze upon a child;
A young bud bursting into blossom;
Artless, as Eve yet unbeguiled,
And agile as a young opossum. [4; *p* 18]

Opossum arrives with an impact that, after the first moment of amusement, seems nothing less than the discovery of a hidden truth. The last word of the stanza completes a pleasant verbal equation: as *artless* is to *agile*, so *a young bud* is to *a young opossum*. The romantic and the realistic views of childhood are clinched in these phrases, but realism scores the comic triumph. To the reader, such felicitous turns of comic rhyme may well bear the appearance of haphazard winnings in some phonetic lucky dip. *Blossom* might seem almost to defy the prediction of an acceptable rhyming partner. The obvious expedient is a rough-and-ready phrasal rhyme (*eg*: *across 'em*), round which a tolerable piece of doggerel could be turned ; but the gifted practitioner ignores the obvious and plans for the frankly improbable, concluding his stanzaic business as calmly and decisively as though the issue of finding a rhyme had never for a moment been in doubt. The rhyme falls pat, and *almost* unpredictably – almost, because there are semantic tremors in the text, giving brief forewarning; the first palpable shock-waves of the oncoming rhyme begin to touch us with *agile*.

(b) The rarity of feminine rhyme

There are quite severe constraints on rhyming in English, particularly on the occurrence of feminine rhyme. Masculine rhymes are reasonable plentiful, except when the vowel of a rhyming syllable is short . Syllables ending in a long vowel or a diphthong (*eg*: *sea*, *sky*, *day*) attract a fairly large number of rhymes; limitations begin to be felt when the vowel is followed by a consonant or consonant cluster, and are notably apparent when a short vowel is followed by two or more consonants. (For the word *glimpsed* it is difficult to find a rhyme.) A few masculine rhymes are grossly overworked (*moon-June*, *mouse-house, breath-death, sky-fly: etc*), to the extent that we begin to presume the existence of a semantic kinship between the tired old rhyming partners: a *mouse* belongs in a *house*, as *breath* is the antonymic counterpart of *death*, as *sky* is your only place to *fly*.

Feminine rhymes are not so easily come by, and on occasion enforce either the yoking of unlikely partners (*eg*: *beholders – moulders*), or the rhyming of a word against a phrase (*eg*: *began her – manner*). (The examples are taken from Browning's poem, *Women as Roses*.) The serious poet must try to avoid both the tendency towards banality in masculine rhyme and the danger of stilted contrivance in the feminine pattern. The business of the humorous writer is quite the reverse. He insists remorselessly on the banal rhyme, by giving prosodic accent even to normally unaccented words, and he sallies recklessly into disyllabic rhyming. Here, by way of illustration, is a passage from *Don Juan*, a work of remarkable stylistic latitude, in which Byron ranges from high romantic lyricism to lowbrow humorous versifying in the knockabout vein. In the episode from which our illustration is taken, Don Juan stands on Shooter's Hill, musing on the prospect of London, capital of the land of liberty. While he is thus engaged, he is attacked by a gang of footpads. The change from romantic philosopher to crude man of action is instant:

Juan yet quickly understood their gesture,
  And being somewhat choleric and sudden,
Drew forth a pocket pistol from his vesture,
  And fired it into one assailant's pudding –
Who fell, as ox rolls o'er in his pasture,
  And roared out, as he writhed his native mud in,
Unto his nearest follower, or henchman,
'O Jack! I'm floored by that 'ere bloody Frenchman!'
[3; *p* 790]

This is doggerel of a strenuous kind, sustained and brought to a triumphant conclusion by those ingenious rhymes, with their varying degrees of predictability. *Gesture – vesture* is a quaint rhyme, while *vesture – pasture* is a quaintly inexact rhyme; but Byron's real skill in rum rhyming is here reserved for the companion set, *sudden*, *pudding* (pronounced 'pudden') and *mud in* (*in* requiring a reduced vowel, as in the final syllable of *raisin*). The claptrap fun of the stanza is crowned with *henchman – Frenchman*, which is humorous not so much because of its oddity, as of its inevitability. There *is* only one exact rhyme for *henchman*. The fact that Juan is a Spaniard makes it all the funnier.

(c) Comic density of rhyme

Density of rhyme, like density of alliteration, is to the English reader either wearisome or downright comic. These densities are a blemish on would-be-serious verse; instead of conveying a passionate intensity, they too often dissipate feeling in harmonic razzmatazz. Swinburne is an example of a poet who over-alliterates; and for over-rhyming, to a ragtime beat, there is no one to match Edgar Allan Poe:

Once upon a midnight dreary, while I pondered weak and
  weary,
Over many a quaint and curious volume of forgotten lore –
While I nodded, nearly napping, suddenly there came a
  tapping,
As of someone gently rapping, rapping at my chamber door,
''Tis some visitor,' I muttered, 'tapping at my chamber door –
  Only this and nothing more.'

Ah, distinctly I remember, it was in the bleak December,
And each separate dying ember wrought its ghost upon the
  floor
Eagerly, I wish'd the morrow; – vainly I had sought to borrow
From my books surcease of sorrow – sorrow for the lost
  Lenore –
For the rare and radiant maiden whom the angels name
  Lenore –
  Nameless here for evermore.

And the silken sad uncertain rustling of each purple curtain
Thrill'd me – fill'd me with fantastic terrors never felt before;
So that now, to still the beating of my heart, I stood
repeating,
''Tis some visitor entreating entrance at my chamber door –
Some late visitor entreating entrance at my chamber door;
This it is, and nothing more.'

This is the opening of Poe's celebrated poem *The Raven*; it continues for fifteen more stanzas in the same elaborately ornamented style, bejewelled with multiple rhyme, crusted with alliteration, inlaid with assonances, loquacious as *Euphues* and nearly as boring. Not surprisingly, the piece has been the subject of many parodies, including a brilliant attack by C. L. Edson, entitled *Ravin's of the Piute Poet Poe*:

Once upon a midnight dreary, eerie, scary,
I was wary, I was weary, full of worry, thinking of my lost
Lenore,
Of my cheery, aery, fairy, fiery Dearie – (Nothing more).
I was napping, when a tapping on the overlapping coping,
woke me, yapping, groping . . . toward the rapping. I went
hopping, leaping . . .
hoping that the rapping on the coping
Was my little lost Lenore.
That on opening the shutter to admit the latter critter, in
she'd flutter from the gutter with her bitter eyes a-glitter;
So I opened wide the door, what was there? The dark weir
and the drear moor – or I'm a liar – the dark mire, the
drear moor, the mere door, and nothing more! [10; *p* 103]

This makes fun not only of Poe's chiming rhyming, but also of his rhythmic romping – as the allusion to the 'Piute' in the title makes plain. Edson has shrewdly perceived in Poe's metres an Indian drum-rhythm (BOOM-boom-boom-boom) like the relentless thumping of Hiawatha prosody.

Dense crowding of rhyme – a name for this lame game? rich rhyme? pack rhyme? shunt rhyme? – characterizes much fun of the family go-one-better variety. In parlours and places where they play Scrabble, exercises like the following are not uncommon:

'*Definition*'	'*Response*'
The Princess of Wales is . . .	Princess Di
And a person appointed to observe the activities of the Princess of Wales is . . .	a Princess Di spy
And a convenience food consumed by a person appointed to observe the activities of the Princess of Wales is . . .	a Princess Di spy pie
And a man who supplies with convenience foods the person appointed to observe the activities of the Princess of Wales is . . .	a Princess Di spy pie guy
And a false report concerning the man who supplies with convenience foods the person appointed to observe the activities of the Princess of Wales is . . .	a Princess Di spy pie guy lie
And a loud exclamation following that false report concerning the man who supplies with convenience foods the person appointed to observe the activities of the Princess of Wales is . . .	a Princess Di spy pie guy lie cry

On the 'definition' side of the running exchanges, the game recalls the syntax of *The House That Jack Built* ('this is the dog that chased the cat that killed the rat', *etc*) On the 'response' side, rhyming words, all nouns, all monosyllables, build sequences that correspond, element by element, with the syntactic chaining of the definition. One side is elaborate, the other laconic, as the game explores the fun of English syntax side by side with the fun of English rhyming.

(d) Humorous rhythms

No rhythm is humorous *per se*, unless one counts the familiar door-knock rhythm with the *sforzando* accent at the close (*boom-diddy-boom-boom,* BOOM-BOOM), but rhythms can become humorous contextually, by virtue of their banality, or their lawlessness, or their residual associations.

A banal rhythm is one that marches exactly, in relentless synchronization, with its governing metre. This makes for one kind of doggerel, the type of the Bellocian 'cautionary tale', or of ruthless rhymes like our 'Little Willie' verse in Chapter 1. It also makes serious verse parodically vulnerable. The unvarying beat of Longfellow's *Hiawatha* has provoked numerous mockeries, *eg*:

When he killed the Mudjokivis,
Of the skin he made him mittens,
Made them with the fur side inside,
Made them with the skin side outside,
He, to get the warm side inside,
Put the inside skin side outside;
He, to get the cold side outside,
Put the warm side fur side inside.
That's why he put fur side inside,
Why he put the skin side outside,
Why he turned them inside outside. [6; *p* 273]

A 'lawless' rhythm is one that accepts or discards metrical rule, as the rhymester's convenience dictates. The rhythms of the mere poetaster may be innocently lawless; those of an accomplished humorist like Ogden Nash are lawless by design. Thus, in his *England Expects*:

Let us pause to consider the English,
Who when they pause to consider themselves they get all
reticently thrilled and tinglish,
Because every Englishman is convinced of one thing, viz:
That to be an Englishman is to belong to the most exclusive
club there is:
A club to which benighted bounders of Frenchmen and
Germans and Italians et cetera cannot even aspire to
belong,
Because they don't even speak English, and the Americans
are worst of all because they speak it wrong.
[6; *p* 181]

Without its rhymes, this might qualify as 'speech rhythm', or as a species of Whitmanesque *vers libre*. Rhymes, however, promote an expectation of regularity in metre; rhyme and metre generally go together, as devices that frame and organize versified discourse. In Ogden Nash's verse the expectation of metrical law is frustrated. There is no metre to dictate the length of the line. Each line is a syntactic unit, a phrase or a clause of complex construction, the complexity often increasing from line to line, so that a discursive gabble is artfully devised; but each gobbet of gabble ends with a rhyme, pulling the reader back to the notion of regularly-timed verse.

Rhythms may be said to be 'residually' humorous if they are strongly reminiscent of an outmoded rhetoric. (Comparably, there are 'residually humorous' objects whose utilitarian status has lapsed: antimacassars, galoshes, chamber-pots.) We have, for example, a Victorian/Edwardian tradition of parlour recitals and music-hall monologues that make intensive use of jaunty, tripping dactylic/anapaestic rhythms, or of a loose-footed trot with several weak syllables pattering after each strong beat:

He was known as 'Mad Carew' by the subs of Khatmandu,
He was hotter than they felt inclined to tell;
But for all his foolish pranks, he was worshipped in the ranks,
And the Colonel's daughter smiled on him as well. [31; *p* 246]

Now, William, I'll prove if you really are true,
For you say that you love me – I don't think you do;
If really you love me you must give up the wine,
For the lips that touch liquor shall never touch mine.
[31; *p* 199]

It is almost certainly the association with such recitals – rhetorical, sentimental, moralizing, 'improving' – that has made the trot-and-peck rhythm residually comic. It persists here and there in the oratory of politicians and labour leaders, but its true legacy is in the language and 'patter' of the stage comedian:

> A funny thing happened on the way to the theatre tonight . . .

> Ladies and gentlemen, ladies and gentlemen, a little recitation, a little recitation entitled She was only an architect's daughter, but she let the borough surveyor.

That such rhythms often strike us as either quaint or jocose is a limitation on their use in serious verse, and inhibits attempts to adapt English to the grand march of Graeco-Roman prosody, as in these lines from C. Day Lewis's poem *A Time to Dance*:

> Sing we the two lieutenants, Parer and M'Intosh,
> After the War wishing to hie them home to Australia,
> Planned they would take a high way, a hazardous crazy air-way:
> Death their foregone conclusion, a flight headlong to failure,
> We said.

The imitation of the classical hexameter is obvious in a line like *Planned they would take a high way, a hazardous crazy air-way*. It is a praiseworthy attempt, yet the dactylic trot unkindly makes Parer and M'Intosh brothers-under-the-skin of Mad Carew and the subs of Khatmandu. (The dignity of the verse, it might be added, is not enhanced by the cockney rhyme of *Australia* and *failure*.)

In comic rhetoric, the trot-rhythm is now and then interrupted by another rhythmic impulse, the emphatic juxtaposition of strong beats:

> Surprising, too, what one can do with a pint of fat black beetles

> What wonderfully blue eyes you have, Earnest! They are quite, quite blue.

> The clerk was a táll, cóol dévĭl.
>
> 'Cóme óut', said the manager, coldly.

W. S. Gilbert and Oscar Wilde furnish the first two examples; the last marks that sublime moment in Leacock's *My Financial Career* when the hapless economist, having gone to the bank to deposit all of sixty-four dollars, seeks a private interview with the manager, and on being dismissed from that august presence walks dazedly into the safe. *'Come out', said the manager, coldly.* The word *coldly* is a master-stroke; but one could write a little essay on this splendid utterance, demonstrating the skill of its phonetic and rhythmic construction. *Come* and *coldly* alliterate; the spondee-rhythm of *Come out* is haltingly mimicked, at the end of the line, in the trochaic fall of *coldly*. The success of this drastically simple turn of phrase is all the more apparent if we try to imagine how the line might have been bungled:

> 'Not that way.' The manager's tones were bleak.

Leacock's version demonstrates beautifully the convergence, on a point of intense comic focus, of alliteration, rhythm, and word-choice.

8.2 FRAMES

Humorous intention is made apparent through the construction of a setting, or frame, which sanctions the joke ('given these conditions, you may laugh') and also suggests an interpretative process. These matters have been discussed elsewhere, notably in Chapters Three and Four, but one or two additional or summarizing comments may be made:

(a) Prosodic frames

Often it is the apparatus of rhythm and rhyme that makes a declaration of comic intent, and in such cases it might almost be said that the prosody *is* the joke; rather as the clown's costume and make-up can legitimize the most feeble or dubious essays in humour. Prosodic dress can transform a sober proposition – for instance, this:

> If you were to introduce a hornet into someone's pocket, it would inflict a very painful sting.

Unfunny material, to say the least of it; but in the hands of W. S. Gilbert it becomes:

> . . . hornets sting like anything, when placed in waistcoat pockets.

We note the rhythm, and how the dactylic stumble on *anything* breaks the trochaic canter of the line; the internal rhyme on *sting* and *anything*; the alliteration of '*p*laced' and '*p*ockets' and the possible assonance of 'pl*a*ced' and 'w*ai*stcoat' (though Gilbert may have said 'wesket'). These devices make a joking costume, an alienating comic mask, for a lugubrious assertion – one of the techniques of humour when its theme is pain, or suffering, or violence, or death. *Never fear,* says the bouncing prosody, *we do but murder in jest, poison in jest.*

Not that prosody is the entire joke in this Gilbertian line, which is an exercise in the humour of assigning factual substance to mere conjecture. The paraphrase suggests that *if you were . . . it would*; but the actual line ignores *if* and *would* and asserts its *do*. We laugh, then, at the implied claim to empirical knowledge in such a particular instance (not *any* pocket, but, specifically, the *waistcoat* pocket). Nevertheless, much is contributed by the metre and rhyming of a line which, in its turn, is related to a larger prosodic scheme:

> A good spring gun breeds endless fun, and makes men jump
> like rockets –
> And turnip heads on posts
> Make very decent ghosts.
> Then hornets sting like anything, when placed in waistcoat
> pockets –
> Burnt cork and walnut juice
> Are not without their use.
> No fun compares with easy chairs whose seats are stuffed with
> needles –
> Live shrimps their patience tax
> When put down people's backs.
> Surprising, too, what one can do with a pint of fat black
> beetles
> And treacle on a chair
> Will make a Quaker swear! [6 *p* 135]

Take one line out of its context, and its rhymes and rhythms might seem casual, faintly-marked, even accidental; the context of other lines establishes these features unmistakably. The rhythmic/rhyming procedures take charge, create expectations (how will he find a rhyme for *needles*?), assume a comic function that excuses the puerility of the content. The jokes are prosodically framed; the prosody gives respectable substance to the jokes.

(b) Syntactic frames

The ordering of elements in a clause, the contrivance of parallel constructions, the imposition of a cohesive syntactic pattern on a sequence of sentences in a text, are all ways of creating, in prose, a frame for comic narrative comparable to the prosodic framing of humorous verse. In the following example, from Saki's story *The Peace of Mowsle Barton*, the syntactic framing is made up of subtle parallels and antitheses:

> Time and space seemed to lose their meaning and their abruptness; the minutes slid away into hours, and the meadows and fallows sloped away into middle distance, softly and imperceptibly. Wild weeds of the hedgerow straggled into the flower-garden, and wallflowers and garden bushes made counter-raids into farmyard and lane. Sleepy-looking hens and solemn preoccupied ducks were equally at home in yard, orchard, or roadway; nothing seemed to belong definitely to anywhere; even the gates were not necessarily to be found on their hinges. And over the whole scene brooded the sense of peace that had almost a quality of magic in it. In the afternoon you felt that it had always been afternoon, and must always remain afternoon; in the twilight you knew that it could never have been anything else but twilight. [21; *p* 90]

The conscious elegance of this hardly requires comment, except to say that in that very quality of *consciousness*, the suggestion of a tutored hand working the prose design, there is a hint of comedy to come. Humour is gently located in the studious counterpoises:

example 1

minutes	slid away	into hours
meadows	sloped away	into the middle distance

example 2

wild weeds of the hedgerow	straggled	into the flower-garden
wallflowers and garden bushes	made counter-raids	into farmyard and lane

In example 1 there is a touch of word-play on the matching verb-adverb constructions (*cf*: *She flew into a temper and flounced into the garden*). In example 2 there is the mildest invitation to smile at the poise of *straggled* and *made counter-raids*, expressions that cast incongruous military shadows across the bland pacific imagery of this rural scene. We may not laugh outright, but if we read sensitively we at least observe the humorous focus, created by a syntactic pattern.

(c) Authorial comment: the 'inquit'

Another kind of frame is created by the author's interventions in the comic narrative, with comment on events and on the behaviour and feelings of his characters. The device called the *formulate* (see Ch. 4) is a type of authorial framing; another is seen in the construction and development of the *inquit* (='he/she said'), the reporting of a speech that often includes some note on the disposition, *etc* of the speaker:

'Come out', said the manager, coldly

The inquit is a kind of stage-direction. The manager's response is scripted; he is required to *say*, not to *snap*, *bark*, or *boom*, and he must say his words *coldly*, rather than *furiously* or *peevishly*. Here is one of the little strings on which the comedian makes his puppets dance. The staging can be more elaborate:

'Come out,' said the manager, his eyes gleaming.
'Come out,' said the manager. His spectacles glittered balefully as he spoke.
'Come out.' The manager spoke in coldly measured tones, his spectacles shining with a cheerless light, like November dawn on a frozen duck-pond.

What the author supplies in such instances is a perspective and colouring, a *direction to view*, which cannot be said to emerge 'naturally' from the progress of events or from the psychology of character. If I write *His spectacles glittered balefully*, I am making an interpretation on my reader's behalf. In other words, I am practising a deceitful intervention. I 'set up' the action and the scene, I 'set up' my character, I 'set up' (in a somewhat different sense) my reader. I, the executant-outside-the-text deal with my respondent via manipulations of the executant-within-the-text. (On these terms, see Ch. 2.7.) The point of these dealings is constantly to adjust the framing of the narrative so as to direct my audience to a required interpretation, of each part and of the whole.

A footnote: in a comic extension of these techniques of authorial commentary, characters in a story or play are allowed to comment 'objectively' on their own actions, motives and involvements. The character, eerily self-aware, is allowed to be his own author:

> 'Come out,' said the manager. 'I hope you notice how coldly measured my tones are. By Jove, yes. Are my glasses glittering balefully? It's only to be expected, you know.'

The objective framing of the narrative is challenged when the characters take over the stage direction. This is potentially funny, but sometimes disturbing, a joke about style suggesting that experience is only style and nothing more. Its implication that people are merely the language they use in the moment of using it, and 'character' an illusion, is perhaps nihilistic, certainly disconcerting; most disconcerting, indeed, when it is at its funniest.

8.3 CONVENTIONAL TROPES: OVERSTATEMENT, UNDERSTATEMENT, COUNTERSTATEMENT

Certain figures are associated conventionally with the management of comic narrative; for example, the comic simile, which designedly strains the proportion between compared objects. Thus Saki, in his story *Adrian*:

> He transformed the bathroom label to the adjoining bedroom door, which happened to be that of Frau Hofrath Schilling, and this morning from seven o'clock onwards the old lady had a stream of involuntary visitors; she was too horrified and scandalized it seems to get up and lock her door. The would-be bathers flew back in confusion to their rooms, and, of

> course, the change of numbers led them astray again, and the corridor gradually filled with panic-stricken, scantily robed humans, dashing wildly about like rabbits in a ferret-infested warren. [21; *p* 56]

Dashing wildly about like rabbits in a ferret-infested warren; the comic point of the simile is hardly its propriety – the customary measure of efficiency in rhetoric – but rather, the deliberate incongruity that exaggeratedly suggests *terror*, in conditions that betoken the lesser evils of bewilderment or mere annoyance. This figure belongs to the comic mode of hyperbole, or overstatement, the stylistic trademark of many a tall tale.

Understatement, which the British are said to cultivate, is a common ironic resort: *Napoleon, who knew a little about musketry*; *One man who enjoyed a snack was Henry VIII*. Counterstatement takes various forms, *eg* that of the oxymoron which I use when I complain that *Some clergymen are aggressively meek*, or some wider form of paradox, such as the remark of a friend who had undergone a long course of psychotherapy, *Psychoanalysis cures the patient beyond all hope of recovery*. Playful paradox runs like a grain through the writings of wits like Oscar Wilde and Saki:

> His baptismal register spoke of him pessimistically as John Henry, but he had left that behind with the other maladies of infancy, and his friends knew him under the front-name of Adrian. His mother lived in Bethnal Green, which was not altogether his fault; one can discourage too much history in one's family, but one cannot always prevent geography. And, after all, the Bethnal Green habit has this virtue – that it is seldom transmitted to the next generation. [21; *p* 53]

This is in fact Saki, but some constructions, in their affectation of a bantering detachment, sound a Wildean note: *one can discourage too much history in one's family, but one cannot prevent geography*. *One* is a significant pronoun here; also significant are the scrupulously and ironically reasonable adverbs – *not altogether*, *too much*, *cannot always, is seldom*. The passage combines the effects of counterstatement (the baptismal register is pessimistic), understatement ('not altogether his fault') and overstatement (for indeed, to imply that a baptismal name is one of the *maladies of infancy* is surely overstating the case).

Overstatement and understatement are major principles of comic staging. A narrator may frame his recital consistently in overstatement; or he may regularly underplay, thereby constructing a different kind of humorous frame and encouraging in his audience a different set of suppositions and anticipations. Counterstatement, as a recurrent device, has the effect of constantly shifting or unsettling the frame, disturbing perspective till the audience is not quite sure how to respond to a narrative. One might ask, for example, whether Saki's ostensible snobbery is (a) an entirely humorous position, never to be taken seriously – 'We merely joke about Bethnal Green, it's a splendid place', or (b) a candidly serious position, humorously reflected upon – 'Well, Bethnal Green is ghastly, isn't it, but at least we can joke about it', or (c) an overtly humorous position with covert hints of seriousness – 'We are only joking, of course, but still, if you care to take it seriously . . .'. This uncertainty is essential to the humorous mischief of Saki; it is the comic mask through which he teases his readers.

8.4 THE PERFORMANCE ELEMENT

A popular song of the 1930s declared to the world that *It ain't what you do, it's the way that you do it*, with the corollary *It ain't what you say, it's the way that you say it*. This applies to humour as much as to anything. Everyone knows that jokes are made or marred in the telling; for which reason, the inexperienced teller accepts and respects formulae handed down to him, seldom daring to attempt variations in the pattern of a locative joke, or to practise improvisations in the structure of an anecdote. Professionals originate and improvise; laymen follow a script.

There is, indeed, a 'performance element' in humour, a histrionic capacity that can raise a chuckling response to material virtually devoid of any distinctively comic feature. A skilled comic actor can read aloud a set of names culled from the telephone catalogue, and by intonations, by exquisitely judged pauses, by sensuous variations of vocal timbre, by a magisterial solemnity of countenance, can make the onlooker smile. Skilled comic actors, however, are seldom required to exercise their arts of interpretation on such unlikely material. As a rule they are provided with scripts into which the notations of humour have been more or less emphatically written by authors concerned with the vocal implications of their writing.

Many details of performance are prepared in the script, so that all that should be required is an intelligent delivery, bringing out the major points of comic import. No script, however, is so exhaustively prepared as to leave nothing to the interpreter, and there is many a literary anecdote that depends on a good performance. For instance:

> Beerbohm Tree, a late representative of the grand old tradition of 'ham' acting, performed with such peculiarity of emphasis that his audiences often suspected him of keeping something stronger than mineral water in his dressing room. One night, when Tree was acting the part of Richard II, this suspicion was so derisively voiced by the gallery that Tree, incensed, paused in mid-performance to march downstage and yell at his accusers, *'Drunk, am I? Wait till you see John of Gaunt!'*

This anecdote is carefully scripted, and its humour is mediated through the structure of a text consisting of two sentences. The first of these states the background to the story, and the second reports the story itself. In the first sentence, the notion of 'hamming', essential to the joke, is suggested in the actual wording, in the periphrases *with such peculiarity of emphasis* ('bawling') and *something stronger than mineral water* ('alcohol') The story about a ham is hammily narrated. These periphrases have an additional role in the patterning of the anecdote, as they artfully avoid the direct statement of notions pointedly formulated in the second sentence (*yell*, *drunk*) The second sentence scripts the feelings and responses of the central figure (*incensed*, *yell*), and with the phrase *acting the part of* – a form of words implying the distinction between player and role – foreshadows the conclusion, in which Tree's fellow actor is perversely and comically identified with the character he plays.

There is thus a great deal in the writing of the text that might be regarded as a performance *in posse*, or as hints for a vocal realization of the anecdote. Nevertheless, some imagination is required to conceive a recital of the piece, and in particular of the closing outburst, *Drunk am I? Wait till you see John of Gaunt*! The difference between merely reading such a text and actually hearing it well performed could be the difference between the abstracted smile and the full-blooded laugh. A performer with the right command of the stage intonation, of the plummy timbre, of the 'peculiarity of emphasis' referred to in the first sentence, might enforce laughter. This is the virtue of performance. Yet the receptive and sympathetic reader can also, in his way, perform, soundlessly reconstructing the sound of the text.

In the last analysis (a phrase which now falls appropriately) the language of humour is powerless without the *speech* of humour. Jokes are *told*; somewhere beyond the text is a voice, telling, delivering, timing. Just as we can never love or understand poetry if it is not heard – heard in the imagination at least, given its phantom performance – so we can never know the bliss of humour until we can recognize its voices. Our commitment to our favourite texts begins when we grasp a way of speaking; the comedian is a poseur, a pedant, a snob, a sentimentalist, an old-fashioned ass, a lumpish provincial, a transatlantic outsider, until we catch an accent and are charmed, until an intonation, wry and engaging, is heard, until the warmth of a companionable tone puts us at ease. Then the text becomes a familiar delight, pleasant by day in the stolen time of the easychair, still more pleasant at night when one is abed and reading, islanded and serene and all-at-home among these voices that coax and chuckle and console. Tell your tale. Speak to me. Make the voices that hold in spell the child with his torch under the blanket, the reader on the train, the housebound woman playing truant from her loneliness. As to what the voices have to say, that may be small matter and frivolous; all the jokes, the puns, the paradoxes, the rhymes and anecdotes, seemingly add little to our knowledge and our stature; they are only human, after all; yet let us consider, let us affirm as a final word, that these things are a spume of the mind, out of which images of transcendent loveliness and wisdom are also born.

Bibliography

This brief bibliography lists items ranging from *The Old Joke Book* to the *Journal of Literary Semantics*, a piquant association that expresses for me something of the oddity of the enterprise. Writings on the language of humour are neither numerous nor easily accessible, and few are directly concerned with humour and style; in consequence, it is hardly possible to produce the sort of bibliography that might be said to be coherently representative of an argument.

Section (i) cites literary sources substantially quoted in my text, and mentions some collections, anthologies, etc, which have provided me with an illustration here and there. Section (ii) lists books and articles on humour, together with a miscellany of works that I have found to be in some way relevant to the structure, philosophy, and pragmatics of humorous discourse.

(i) Literary Sources

1 Ahlberg, Janet and Allan (1978) *The Old Joke Book*, Fontana Lion Books: London.
2 Ahlberg, Janet and Allan (1982) *The Ha Ha Bonk Book*, Puffin Books: London.
3 Byron, George Gordon, Lord (1952 edn) *The Poetical Works of Lord Byron*, Oxford University Press: London.
4 Calverley, C. S. (1974 edn) *The English Poems of Charles Stuart Calverley*, Spear, H. D. (ed.), Leicester University Press: Leicester.
5 Carroll, Lewis (1975 edn) *Alice's Adventures in Wonderland* and *Through the Looking Glass* in Martin Gardner (ed.), *The Annotated Alice*, Penguin Books: London.
6 Cohen, J. M. (ed.) (1952) *The Penguin Book of Comic and Curious Verse*, Penguin Books: London.
7 Cunningham, Bronnie (1974) *The Puffin Joke Book*, illustrated by Quentin Blake, Puffin Books: London.
8 Dickens, Charles (1948 edn) *Bleak House*, New Oxford Illustrated Dickens, Oxford University Press: London
9 Dickens, Charles (1969 edn) *Pickwick Papers* (*The Posthumous Papers of the Pickwick Club*), Oxford University Press: London.
10 Falk, Robert Paul (ed.) (1975) *The Antic Muse: American Writers in Parody*, Grove: New York.

11 Forster, John (repr. 1972) *Life of Jonathan Swift*, John Murray: London; repr. Folcroft Library Editions.
12 Gilbert, Sir W. S. (1932 edn) *Plays and Poems of W. S. Gilbert*, with a preface by Deems Taylor, Random House: New York.
13 Graves, Robert (1951) *Poems and Satires, 1951*, Cassell: London.
14 Graves, Robert (1955) *The Crowning Privilege*, Cassell: London.
15 Harte, Bret (1900) *The Complete Works*, Vol. V, Chatto & Windus: London.
16 Heller, Joseph (1980 edn) *Good as Gold*, paperback repr. Corgi Books: London.
17 Jerome, Jerome K. (1980 edn) *Three Men in a Boat*, Penguin Books: London.
18 Laing, R. D. (1973) *Knots*, Penguin Books: London.
19 Larkin, Philip (1955) *The Less Deceived*, The Marvel Press: London.
20 Leacock, Stephen (1973 edn) *The Bodley Head Leacock*, Priestly, J. B. (ed.), The Bodley Head: London.
21 Munro, H. H. (Saki) (1981 edn) *The Best of Saki*, Tom Sharpe (ed.), Picador: London.
22 Nash, Ogden (1952) *The Face is Familiar*, J.M. Dent: London
23 Rees, Nigel (1978) *Quote-Unquote*, George Allen and Unwin: London.
24 Rees, Nigel (1979) *Graffiti Lives, O. K.*, George Allen and Unwin: London.
25 Rees, Nigel (1981) *Graffiti 3*, George Allen and Unwin: London.
26 Squire, J. C. (1900; volume undated) *Collected Parodies*, Hodder and Stoughton: London.
27 Squire, J. C. (1929) *Apes and Parrots: an Anthology of Parodies*, Jenkins: London.
28 Tennyson, Alfred Lord (1969 edn) *The Poems of Tennyson*, Christopher Ricks (ed.), Longman: London.
29 Thurber, James (1963 edn) *Lanterns and Lances*, Penguin Books: London.
30 Tidwell, James Nathan (ed.) (1956) *A Treasury of American Folk Humor*, Crown: New York.
31 Turner, Michael P. (ed.) (1974) *Parlour Poetry: A Casquet of Gems*, Pan Books: London.
32 Waterhouse, Keith (1963 edn) *Billy Liar*, Penguin Books: London.
33 Waugh, Evelyn (1980 edn) *Decline and Fall*, Penguin Books: London.

(ii) Books, articles, etc on humour, or relevant to the study of humorous language

34 Austin, J. L. (1976) *How To Do Things With Words*, Urmson J. O. and Sbisa, Marina (eds.), Oxford University Press: London.
35 Bergson, Henri (1980 edn and transln) *Le rire: Essai sur la signification du comique*, transl. as *Laughter* in Sypher, Wylie (ed.), *Comedy*, Johns Hopkins University Press: Baltimore and London.

36 Brown, James (1956) 'Eight Types of Puns', *PMLA*.
37 Carroll, John B. (1964) *Language and Thought*, Prentice-Hall: Englewood Cliffs, NJ.
38 Carston, Robyn (1981) 'Irony and Parody in the Use-Mention Distinction', *Nottingham Linguistic Circular*, 10, 1.
39 Ching, Marvin K. L. (1980) 'Interpreting Meaningful Nonsense' in Ching, Marvin K. L., Halsey, Michael C. and Lunsford, Ronald F. (eds.), *Linguistic Perspectives on Literature*, Routledge & Kegan Paul: London.
40 Cutler, Anne (1974) 'On saying what you mean without meaning what you say', *Proceedings of the Chicago Linguistic Society*, 10.
41 Eastman, Max (1921) *The Sense of Humour*, Scribner: New York.
42 Eastman, Max (1936) *Enjoyment of Laughter*, Scribner: New York.
43 Farb, Peter (1974) *Word Play: What happens when people talk*, Alfred Knopf: New York.
44 Gnutzmann, Claus, and Kohring, Klaus (1981) *Learning English Humor, I*, Anglistik und Englischunterricht 15, VWT Wissenschaftlicher Verlag: Trier.
45 Grice, H. P. (1975) 'Logic and Conversation' in Cole, P. and Morgan, J. (eds.), *Syntax and Semantics 3*: *Speech Acts*, Academic Press: New York.
46 Grice, H. P. (1978) 'Further Notes on Logic and Conversation' in Cole, P. (ed.), *Syntax and Semantics 9: Pragmatics*, Academic Press: New York.
47 Hancher, Michael (1980) 'How to Play Games with Words: Speech-Act Jokes', *Journal of Literary Semantics*, IX/1.
48 Heller, L. G. (1974) 'Toward a General Typology of the Pun', *Language and Style*, 7.
49 Highet, Gilbert (1962) *The Anatomy of Satire*, Princeton University Press: Princeton, NJ.
50 Johnson, Ragnar (1978) 'Jokes, Theories, Anthropology', *Semiotica*, 22.
51 Kelly, L. G. (1971) 'Punning and the Linguistic Sign', *Linguistics*, 66.
52 Martinich, A. P. (1981) 'A Theory of Communication and the Depth of Humour', *Journal of Literary Semantics*, X/1.
53 Meredith, George (1877, repr. 1980) 'An Essay on Comedy', repr. in Sypher, Wylie (ed.), *Comedy*, Johns Hopkins University Press: Baltimore and London.
54 Milner, G. B. (1972) 'Homo ridens. Towards a Semiotic Theory of Laughter', *Semiotica*, 5.
55 Muecke, D. C. (1970) *Irony*, Methuen: London.
56 Munro, D. H. (1951) *Argument of Laughter*, Cambridge University Press: Cambridge and Melbourne.
57 Osgood, C. E., Suci, G. J. and Tannenbaum, P. H. (1957) *The Measurement of Meaning*, University of Illinois Press: Urbana.
58 Partridge, Eric (1950) 'The Nonsense Words of Lewis Carroll' in *Here, There and Everywhere*, Hamish Hamilton: London.
59 Pirandello, Luigi (1974 edn and transln) *On Humor*, introduced, translated and annotated by Illiano, A. and Teste, D.P., University of North Carolina Studies in Comparative Literature: Chapel Hill, NC.

60 Pospesel, Howard (1974) *Propositional Logic: Introduction to Logic*, Prentice-Hall: Englewood Cliffs, NJ.
61 Pospesel, Howard (1976) *Predicate Logic: Introduction to Logic*, Prentice-Hall: Englewood Cliffs, NJ.
62 Quirk, R., Greenbaum, Š., Leech, G. and Svartvik, J. (1972) *A Grammar of Contemporary English*, Longman: London and New York.
63 Schweizer, Werner Rudolph (1964) *Der Witz*, Francke: Bern.
64 Searle, John R. (1969) *Speech Acts. An Essay in the Philosophy of Language*, Cambridge University Press: London.
65 Searle, John R. (1979) *Expression of Meaning: Studies in the Theory of Speech Acts*, Cambridge University Press: London.
66 Sewell, Elizabeth (1952) *The Field of Nonsense*, Chatto and Windus: London.
67 Sherzer, Joel (1978) 'Oh! That's a pun and I didn't mean it', *Semiotica*, 22.
68 Sully, J. (1902) *Essay on Laughter; its Forms, its Causes, its Development and its Value*, Longmans & Co: London.
69 Sutherland, Robert D. (1970) *Language and Lewis Carroll*, Mouton: The Hague.
70 Wilson, Deirdre (1975) *Presupposition and Non-Truth-Conditional Semantics,* Academic Press: London.

Index